Ethnic Groups in History Textbooks

Ethnic Groups in History Textbooks

Nathan Glazer
Reed Ueda

Ethics and Public Policy Center
Washington, D.C.

Library of Congress Cataloging in Publication Data
Glazer, Nathan.
  Ethnic groups in history textbooks.
  Includes index.
   1. United States—History—Text-books.
  2. Minorities—United States—Study and teaching.
  3. Text-book bias—United States. I. Ueda, Reed.
II. Title.
E175.85.G56   1983   305.8'00973   82-24267
ISBN 0-89633-064-8 (pbk.)

$4.00

Contents

Foreword

UNTIL A COUPLE OF DECADES AGO, American history textbooks tended to ignore the cultural pluralism of American society. This situation has changed, however, and some observers now think that textbooks are devoting too much space to ethnic and racial minorities.

In the following pages Nathan Glazer and Reed Ueda examine six popular high school American history texts with two main questions in view: (1) How do they deal with American diversity? (2) Do they give so much attention to ethnic groups that the main lines of American history are blurred or distorted?

The authors' detailed analysis and conclusions will be of value to all who are concerned about our schools, and especially to parents, school administrators, and teachers. One may hope, too, that the teams engaged in "textbook development" —writers, consultants, publishers' editors, and publishers' market researchers—will glean useful insights from this careful study.

Nathan Glazer is professor of education and sociology at Harvard University and co-editor of *The Public Interest.* He is the author and co-author of numerous books, including *The Lonely Crowd* (with David Riesman and Reuel Denney), *American Judaism, Beyond the Melting Pot* (with Daniel P. Moynihan), and *Affirmative Discrimination: Ethnic Inequality and Public Policy.*

Reed Ueda is assistant professor of history at Tufts University and was a research editor for the *Harvard Encyclopedia of American Ethnic Groups.* He is the author of "Suburban Social Change and Educational Reform" (in *Social Science History,* 3 [1979], 167-203) and other articles on ethnic and educational questions.

This is the third analysis of high school textbooks published by the Ethics and Public Policy Center. Preceding it were *Values in an American Government Textbook: Three Appraisals* by Michael Novak, Jeane Kirkpatrick, and Anne Crutcher, and *How the Cold War Is Taught: Six American History Textbooks Examined* by Martin F. Herz.

Several essays in the Center's reprint series bear on contemporary educational problems, including *Patterns of Black Excellence* by Thomas Sowell, *Washington vs. the Public Schools* by J. Myron Atkin, *Christian Schools, Racial Quotas, and the I.R.S.* by Peter Skerry, and *Education, Character, and American Schools* by Gerald Grant.

In all Center publications, the authors alone are responsible for the facts selected and the views expressed.

RAYMOND ENGLISH, Vice President
Ethics and Public Policy Center

Washington, D.C.
February 10, 1983

CHAPTER ONE

Looking at Textbooks

WHAT ARE OUR CHILDREN being taught about minorities in the United States and about the various ethnic strands that make up the American population?

This has been a recurrent concern of those who have examined and reexamined the American textbook over the last fifty years. But during the course of these years, the nature of that concern has shifted. Until recently, the main worry was that textbooks might be teaching prejudiced and discriminatory attitudes; or that, by ignoring ethnic and racial minorities, textbooks were depriving them of their proper role in the shaping of American life. These were the chief concerns, for example, of Michael B. Kane, who examined a group of textbooks in a study sponsored by the Anti-Defamation League of B'nai B'rith (*Minorities in Textbooks: A Study of Their Treatment in Social Studies Texts,* Quadrangle Books, 1970).

But by 1970, things were already changing. The rise of a powerful movement urging racial pride in the largest American minority, the blacks, followed by similar movements in other ethnic and racial groups, led to a new concern: Were American history textbooks distorting the treatment of minorities by devoting too much space to their troubles and achievements, and by exaggerating the degree to which American racial and ethnocentric attitudes and behavior harmed them? This was the major concern of Frances FitzGerald when she wrote her widely reviewed study of American textbooks, *America Revised* (Little, Brown, 1979).

1

To many, the idea that textbooks might be biased toward minorities would seem outlandish. Is it not true that Americans imported and enslaved blacks, subjected them even after slavery to segregation and discrimination, treated Indians cruelly until relatively recently, passed laws penalizing Chinese and Japanese until recent years, subjected Jews to anti-Semitism, and the like? And should not textbooks tell the story?

But there is also another story to tell: That this country has accepted more immigrants, of more varied stocks, than any other nation in the world, and continues to do so; that it has been a beacon for immigrants, despite their knowledge of the prejudiced and discriminatory attitudes and the official discrimination they would find here; that it presents the world with what is probably the most successful example of a complex, modern, multi-ethnic society; and that it goes further than any other great nation in creating a partnership of varied peoples, all of whom are guaranteed a range of rights and offered full participation in the common life of the nation.

Admittedly, the assessment we have just made of a complex situation could be argued with, and indeed it is argued with by those who concentrate on the racist, discriminatory, and crudely assimilating features of American society and government. But we place it at the beginning of our analysis of the treatment of minorities in American history textbooks in order to suggest our view of the kind of balanced judgment that should emerge from the study of the history of the United States.

As we have suggested, if the concern of 1970 was whether minorities and ethnic groups were receiving fair and adequate treatment, the concern of the 1980s—as we can see from *America Revised*—is whether the growing sophistication of publishers in accommodating to every possible pressure group will lead to a Balkanization of American history, in which every group may get a "proper" share, but in which the central story, one in which all groups participate, is simply left aside to be assembled as well as possible by the student and teacher.

This is the question we have addressed in this brief study. But as anyone who has tried to answer the question "what are American history textbooks like today" knows, it is no simple matter to do so, and our answer, because of a very partial coverage, must be a partial one. This is a far more modest exploration than that of Bessie Pierce in 1930 (*Civic Attitudes in American School Textbooks,* University of Chicago Press), who reviewed no fewer than 97 histories, 67 texts in civics and in sociological and economic problems, 45 geographies, and 190 other texts. It is a more partial answer than that of Frances FitzGerald, who had the very valuable idea of looking over textbooks in time to see how they had changed, and who lists no fewer than 111 texts in her bibliography, of which 24 are contemporary American history texts. Our sample is a mere six American history texts, and it is not easy to say how extensively used they are. They are, however, the texts of major textbook publishers, and, unless they have suffered some peculiar disaster, they ought to be in wide use.*

THE SIX TEXTBOOKS

The books we examined are:

Herbert J. **Bass** and others, *Our American Heritage.* Silver Burdett, 1979.

Gerald **Leinwand,** *The Pageant of American History.* Allyn and Bacon, 1975.

Glenn M. **Linden** and others, *A History of Our American Republic.* Laidlaw Brothers (A Division of Doubleday), 1979.

Norman K. **Risjord** and Terry L. Haywoode, *People and Our Country.* Holt, Rinehart and Winston, 1978.

James P. **Shenton** and others, *These United States.* Houghton Mifflin, 1978.

Lewis Paul **Todd** and Merle Curti, *Rise of the American Nation.* Harcourt, Brace, Jovanovich, 1977.

---

*After completing this manuscript we learned of a doctoral thesis, *Conceptions of Citizenship and Nationality in American High School History Textbooks, 1913-1977,* by Micheline Fedyck (Columbia University, 1979). This is an impressive and thorough work, covering many textbooks published over a period of almost two-thirds of a century. It describes changes in the treatment of, among others, blacks, and various groups of immigrants, and analyzes in particular the melting pot and cultural pluralism as contrasting theories of American nationality. Unfortunately, we learned of the thesis too late to make use of it in this study.

We will refer to the books by the name of the principal author, as Bass, Leinwand, Linden, Risjord, Shenton, and Todd.

The variety of history textbooks in print and in use is indicated by the fact that only one of our group of six is in Frances FitzGerald's group of twenty-four. We can reduce the significance of that lack of equivalence by pointing out that she was concerned with elementary school history texts too; we were not. We limited ourselves to the high school level. We feel this is a fair sample, and one that gives a good sense of the range of texts in use for teaching high school students around the country. While our findings would undoubtedly be somewhat different with a different sample, we do not feel they would be very different.

One reason we say this is that clearly our textbooks are designed to appeal to a wide range of high schools around the country; both in content and format they are more like one another than they are different. A certain format has emerged for the high school history text, and while there are variations, it is hard to find any that diverge much from this received format.

The Similarities

All the books in our group have just about the same number of pages, ranging from 726 to 842. Each has a large, double-column format, with many pictures (many of which are in color), many maps and charts, and varied typographic devices to heighten attention to one or another point or detail. They vary in the colorfulness of typographic devices, with some using dazzling colored stars, pointing hands, colored rules, or colored type. All seem to have been influenced by *Sesame Street,* in that they expect attention to lag unless frequently stimulated, even though they are designed for older students with a longer span of attention. Rarely in any of these books do two facing pages appear with text unbroken by a picture or other graphic device. The number of pictures varies from 319 to 401 in addition to graphs and maps.

Those concerned with what is happening to the teaching of American history will be relieved to know that all six of these texts have the text of the Declaration of Independence and the Constitution, sometimes in an appendix, sometimes in the body of the text, and all treat these documents at length as part of the history of the Revolution and the founding of the nation. All show substantial attention to social and statistical data: Todd, for example, charts (in an appendix) changes in the rate of population increase, family income, home ownership, and educational achievement; Linden furnishes graphs on the changing distribution of wealth in the American population; Leinwand charts the immigration flows from 1823 to 1973, trends in population of major cities, and changing levels of black and white income. The texts thus assume that a knowledge of basic social trends in American history is fundamental.

In contrast, the direct narrative account, particularly of wars and battles and leaders, is scanted. So, too, in the content of the pictures, we see few battles and leaders, and many more pictures of common people in the various roles of life: Indians in their villages, immigrants on tenement stoops, free blacks in a northern city church, smiling Japanese-American soldiers in World War II huddling together in a foxhole. Many pictures have been chosen to demonstrate racial minorities and whites working or acting together: a black worker picketing with white organizers, an Asian studying with whites in a citizenship class for naturalization, Mexicans helping Texans defend the Alamo.

Characteristically, these texts are not the product of a single author, except for one (Leinwand), though one must assume that even in that case a group of unnamed editors and consultants played a key role in shaping the text, choosing the pictures and maps, and helping to determine the approach. All the others involve teams, larger or smaller. The most crowded title page (Risjord) lists two authors, two educational consultants, two historical consultants, a geography consultant, and a reading consultant. Linden has four names on the title page, Bass three—the teacher's edition has four, plus pictures of these and two others who participated. Shenton gives three on the title page, plus an editorial advisor, three consultants, and four teacher advisors on the reverse. Linden has four on the title page, Todd only two. Only three of the six books included in their teams of authors (we count fifteen authors in all) historians working in academic departments of history—represented are Columbia University, Temple University, Southern Methodist University, Clark University, and the University of Wisconsin. Of the remaining authors, two are professors in schools of education, five are or were social studies teachers in secondary schools, one is a college sociology instructor, and one is a graduate student in history.

Twelve of the authors are men, three women. The names suggest a variety of ethnic backgrounds—Anglo-Saxon, Scandinavian, Slavic, and Jewish. One text provides pictures, so we can see that one of the authors is a black woman.

This multiple authorship, and the level of distinction of the authors as historians, places these texts in striking contrast to the classic American history texts of the early twentieth century, when Willis Mason West, Albert Bushnell Hart, Andrew C. McLaughlin, Wilbur Fisk Gordy, and Charles and Mary Beard, all leading historians, placed their new interpretations of American history directly into their textbooks. (Merle Curti, the original author of Todd and Curti, was a historian comparable in stature to these.)

In the four books that list consultants, educational administrators and social studies teachers working at the grass roots dominate. We find ten social studies teachers, ten educational administrators, three professors of education, and two academic historians. Twelve of the twenty-six are women, two Japanese, three Hispanic, an undetermined number blacks; their present affiliations cover the country geographically.

Not much is distinctive and individual in these texts. Language in particular is homogenized, and one assumes all the books have gone through the process of editing described by Frances FitzGerald, the purpose of which is to make them acceptable to a wide variety of school boards.

To use our arbitrary alphabetical ordering by principal author:
Bass is rather elementary in language. He begins chapter one with the sentence, "In the year 1516, an Englishman named Sir Thomas More wrote a book called *Utopia*. The book was about a society that Sir Thomas created in his imagination. Everyone has

an opportunity to live a good and happy life." And so on. This tone never weakens.

Can one detect in this volume a distinctive political tone? Perhaps. For example, the treatment of the 1920s begins with a description of "The Economic Boom" and deals with the rise of the auto industry, the electrical industry, chemicals, and advertising. After two-and-a-half descriptive pages come five-and-a-half basically critical ones, with some of the subheads reading "Prosperity—But not for all," "Hail to big business!," "The decline of unions," "Big business gets bigger," "Critics of the New Era," "Mass production—at a cost"; the section ends with a concern that advertising, drawing on modern psychology, was turning human beings into "objects to be moved about like pieces on a chessboard." And further: "Some wondered whether democracy would any longer have meaning when office holders and candidates could slyly change public opinion with advertising techniques" (p. 528). The same fear exists, of course, fifty years later, but one doubts that candidates or office holders ever had the confidence Bass's version attributes to them. The section ends with the great still from *Modern Times* of Charlie Chaplin caught in the wheels of a monstrous machine.

Bass, uniquely, groups all reform movements, from the 1830s to the New Deal, in one of the ten major divisions of the text, breaking the chronological pattern, which suggests that he wants to place greater emphasis on reform, and the evils against which it was directed, than other texts do. This liberal tone undoubtedly is one reason why Bass is also unique in the large amount of space he gives to European immigrants. (We will look at these space allocations in chapter two.) Indeed, another one of the ten units of the book is devoted entirely to immigration. Bass stands out in the amount of information he provides on American immigration, the sources of American diversity, and the problems of adaptation.

Leinwand is if anything even more elementary than Bass. His first sentence, after two paragraphs of introductory text, is, "An immigrant is one who leaves the place where he was born to settle in another country." He also stands second only to Bass in the attention he gives to the European immigrant experience, ahead of Bass in the space devoted to blacks and Indians. One suspects that the sole author's New York City education and experience (degrees from N.Y.U. and Columbia, professor and dean at Baruch College of the City University of New York) must be one reason for this emphasis. The very first chapter is entitled "The Immigrant Experience" and has pictures of Indians and 1912 immigrants to New York on facing pages. In this volume, every subhead is a question, from the first, "Why Do People Become Immigrants?," down to (to quote some of the question-subheads of the last chapter): "Is All Change Progress?" "Will the Population Bomb Explode?" "Is Ours a Violent Society?" "Is Ours a Corrupt Society?" "Why Drugs?" "Should Women Be Liberated?" And finally, "Abundance for What?"

Leinwand and Bass are the most elementary in language of the six texts, are the most progressive or liberal in political tone, and devote the most space to immigrants and minorities. Whether there is any necessary association among these features we will consider later.

Linden is written in a somewhat less elementary style. It is perhaps reflective of the locations of the four listed authors (Austin, Dallas, Seattle, and Manassas Park, Virginia) that somewhat less space is devoted to reform movements, immigrants, and blacks than in our other texts—and rather more to Indians. Difficult as it is to draw a conclusion as to political tendency in these texts, one does see here hints of conservatism. For example, there is somewhat greater attention to criticism of the New Deal. One heading reads, surprisingly, "The New Deal and the Constitution." (While all the texts discuss Roosevelt's conflict with the Supreme Court, the others do not see a constitutional conflict.) Another reads, "Challenging the Tennessee Valley Authority." Linden treats Senator Joseph McCarthy under the heading "The threat of communism at home," and this is just about the least negative treatment of McCarthy. (For some other headings: Bass, "Cold-War Politics," "The Search for Subversives," and "McCarthyism"; Leinwand, "How Did McCarthyism Endanger America?"; Risjord, "The Second Red Scare," "Truman Hunts Communists," "The Phenomenon of McCarthyism," "America's Fears and Prejudices"; Shenton, "Another Postwar Red Scare," "Internment without trial," "I have a list of names"; Todd is as neutral as Linden.) One senses the same political stance in the treatment of the Vietnam War: for Linden, compared to most of our other authors, it was rather more markedly a war against Communist aggression.

Risjord is typographically the flashiest of our books, and not so elementary in language as Bass and Leinwand. Midwest progressivism plays a larger role. Thus Robert La Follette, who scarcely makes an appearance in our other texts, makes many appearances here (Risjord is a professor at the University of Wisconsin), and the "Wisconsin Idea" gets more than a page, as against more modest or no appearances in the other texts. It is satisfying to see that regionalism still plays some role in American textbooks. The prevailing tone in Risjord is moderate liberal. Few tears are shed over the collapse of Vietnam, as against Linden, who sees it as a tragic loss to Communism.

Shenton is the most sophisticated graphically of the texts, and perhaps the one that most retains a distinctiveness of style. He does not seem afraid of connectives between sentences, and has fewer flat declarative sentences. Shenton is also perhaps the most "with it," beginning, surprisingly, not with the English or the Indians but with the environment: "In the beginning the land was clean. Clear water washed the shores of Lake Michigan and Lake Erie and plunged over Niagara Falls." The first chapter opens with a quote from Seneca's *Medea,* neither otherwise identified—few of our other authors would risk this.

Shenton may be, all in all, and despite its concern with environment, the most upbeat of the texts. The conclusion is the most optimistic. Even after describing the fouling of air, water, and land, Shenton can write, "But technology, at a price, could make the rivers clean again, the air pure again, and the nights and days quiet again," and he continues, under the subtitle "A mighty gift": "The

United States is the oldest of Republics and the first of democracies. To each generation goes the task of making the Union more perfect, a bit better than when it was received, and a happier place for all. . . . For as Abraham Lincoln said of an earlier time, 'It is in your hands, fellow citizens, that the future of the Republic rests.' "

Finally, **Todd** is the densest of the six volumes, and in some ways the most traditional. It has the smallest type, the most narrative, and certainly the highest number of facts, and it eschews the overly simplified language of Leinwand and Bass. In its more sober way, it is nearly as upbeat in its conclusions as Shenton.

SOME OTHER TEXTBOOKS

Admittedly, a wider survey of textbooks than we have conducted here would be desirable. Concerned with the possibility that our original choices were idiosyncratic, we looked at others. Some were very similar, in all the ways described, to our six; examples are Henry W. Bragdon and Samuel P. McCutchen, *History of Free People* (Macmillan, 1978; first published in 1954), and Bernard A. Weisberger, *The Impact of Our Past: A History of the United States* (Webster Division, McGraw Hill, 1976; first published in 1972). We found other books that break with the pattern of text we have been discussing, that raise different questions and give different answers. There are, for example, two-volume texts by major historians that may be used in high schools and community colleges but are more typically used in colleges, or in good private preparatory schools.

Two high school texts are quite out of the ball park defined by the texts we have discussed. The first is *As It Happened*, by Charles G. Sellers, senior author, and Henry Mayer, Edward L. Paynter, Alexander Saxton, Neil L. Shumsky, and Kent Smith (Webster Division, McGraw Hill, 1975). While it looks somewhat like the other high school texts, with its two-column format, its many pictures, its length, and its inserted questions to prod students, its approach puts it into a completely different league. It is primarily document-based, and while quotations are somewhat modernized, they are presented fairly straightforwardly with many difficult and archaic words and old-fashioned spellings. The book is an attempt to put the "jackdaw" approach—in which documents are selected from which the student reconstructs history, supposedly as historians do it—between covers.

Now of course textbook writers reconstruct history not from primary documents but from secondary and tertiary accounts (and from other textbooks). The heavy use of original documents makes this text distinctive. The author makes it clear that inevitably these documents are selected to make a point:

> . . . [T]he authors of this book must frankly admit one difficulty. Obviously you cannot, like the professional historian, spend the time to track down and study the multitude of sources from American history that have survived. . . . [T]he authors have had to select only a handful of the most important sources for each subject studied.
>
> The problem with this is that your conclusions are influenced by the sources available to you. . . . [H]ow can you be sure that authors of this book have not put in sources leading to one conclusion, while leaving out sources that might have led to another conclusion?
>
> The honest answer is that this is hard to avoid completely when limited space is available. . . . But the authors do assure you that they have tried as honestly as possible not to select sources that push you toward one conclusion rather than another [p. 5].

That is somewhat disingenuous. While the authors do eschew conclusions in their own words, their selections lead to clear answers—and in situations where other answers might be given.

As It Happened is also unique in the amount of space it devotes to minorities and immigrants. Chapter five gives twenty-five pages of documents on the American Indian, from the first meeting in Virginia to Western warfare, emphasizing the same themes as the texts we will deal with—expulsion and massacre—but with a detail that is foreign to them. Slavery is given more than eighty pages of documents. In a chapter entitled "The New Arrivals," two sections of sixteen pages document the changing image and social and economic progress of the Irish, from immigrant arrival to the presidency of John F. Kennedy. A twenty-six-page chapter is devoted to "The Jews on New York's Lower East Side," and a twenty-seven-page chapter to "Institutionalized Discrimination," with lengthy sections on the internment of the Japanese Americans, "The Administration of Justice—The Case of the Mexican Americans," and "Economic Opportunity—The Case of Construction Craft Unions and Black Americans."

These are truly exceptional space allocations for American history texts. Irish, Jews, Japanese Americans, Mexican Americans, not to mention discrimination in trade unions against blacks, are generally dealt with, if at all, in fragments of sentences, or at the most paragraphs, in the volumes we will examine.

The political orientation of *As It Happened* is, despite its initial disclaimers, rather clear—and strongly on the left. Its central concern is with equality in American life. Its first chapter is entitled "Status—Why Start With This Idea?" and deals with sumptuary laws in Massachusetts, which it traces back to English feudalism. The theme of equality is a constant—it is the title of the next to last chapter of the book, whose subdivisions deal with income, minorities, and cities and suburbs. There is a strong base in sociological concepts and in economic data; the ideological stance is clear.

Another text we reviewed that stands apart from the dominant one-volume American history is *The American Adventure* (Allyn and Bacon, 1975). Though intended for eighth grade, it is not in any obvious way more simply written than the other texts we looked at. It bears no author's name on the title page, which reads, "Prepared by the Social Science Staff of the Educational Research Council of America." Many names are listed on the reverse of the title page, but they are not identified, and it is not clear how many are historians or social studies teachers. A managing editor is listed (Agnes M. Michnay), an editor-in-chief (Mary Catherine McCarthy), and a director (Raymond English), and they, too, are not further identified.* Its publication was supported by a number of foundations, which are listed; some of them are conservative. *The*

---

*Mr. English, who was then with the Educational Research Council of America, is now vice president of the Ethics and Public Policy Center.—ED.

American Adventure is an assembled product, as most texts are, but it is disconcerting not to be able to refer to it by an author's name, even if that author was not really the author.

This text is in two volumes, which means it has roughly 50 per cent more space at its disposal than the one-volume texts. It resembles our one-volume texts in level of language (simple) and in its colorful double-column format with many pictures, maps, and tables. But it, like Sellers, is interested in challenging students to think; it wants to present history as a subject not with foreordained answers but invested with many controversies, and a good part of its space is devoted to questions. These are not the rather rhetorical questions of Leinwand but questions designed to challenge students. It thus shares with Sellers an approach intended to make the students work (though not as hard as Sellers does, with its original documents).

Also, like Sellers, this text devotes a truly surprising amount of space to racial and minority groups. In part, this is simply because it is longer. But that is clearly not the whole story. There are no fewer than forty pages on the original inhabitants of the territory that became the United States and their descendants, the American Indians; the settling and expansion of Mexico and the settling of Puerto Rico are treated as part of the colonial peopling of the United States; and the text concludes with an extensive and thoughtful chapter on "The Peoples of America." If we were to include this volume in our review, it would stand apart for the detail it provides.

If these two texts defined the future of the treatment of ethnicity and minorities in American textbooks, they would merit extended examination. Alas, it is the brief and elementary treatment of the six texts we have chosen that is overwhelmingly dominant.

CHAPTER TWO

How Much Space For Minorities?

WE HAVE EXAMINED THESE TEXTS from one perspective: How do they handle ethnic and minority issues in American history? How do they deal with American diversity? And: Have we moved from a situation in which blacks, Indians, immigrants, and white and Asian ethnic groups were ignored or patronized, to one in which they receive so much attention—in response to the revolutionary changes of the later 1960s and 1970s—that the main lines of America's common history are submerged? No simple answer will suffice, but our judgment is that the treatment of minorities and ethnic groups is still a surprisingly modest part of these history texts (modest at least in terms of our expectations), and that the issue that should concern us now is how American diversity is handled, rather than that American history has been parceled out among contending minority and ethnic groups.

One way of giving the overall picture is through the stated objectives of our texts. These may be platitudinous and abstract, and yet they do give us some sense of what the authors see as important. For example, Linden tells us that the study of history enables one "to gain an understanding of how the present came to be," and supplies guidelines for action to improve the world (p. 12). Leinwand hopes to acquaint each person with the skills of historical interpretation, to help "students to gain some experience with the tools and the techniques of the historian and to experience some of the excitement that comes from discoveries that one makes oneself" (Preface).

Other texts set as a central purpose promoting knowledge of the process by which a variety of ethnic groups, each with a unique culture, fused into an American nation. Bass states that his principal objective is to explore the "perennially relevant and intriguing question, What makes Americans American?" (Bass, T5). Thus Bass examines the characteristics "associated with the very essence of Americanness," "beliefs such as those in limited government and in progress, attributes such as ethnic diversity and mobility." Risjord, aside from the common goal of giving students an understanding of American democratic ideals, takes as one purpose developing an "appreciation of ways in which a unique American culture developed and was influenced by a variety of nonwestern cultures" (*Teacher's Guide*, p. 11). Shenton also emphasizes as a goal a recognition of "the pluralistic nature of American society" (*Instructor's Guide*, p. 1): "The black experience is traced from colonial times through the Reconstruction period to the civil rights struggle. . . . American Indians are shown as the original inhabitants of the land and in succeeding chapters their generally tragic dealings with the white settlers are recounted. . . . The difficulties of Spanish-speaking Americans are shown, as are the tragedies and triumphs of European immigrants."

Reflecting the Times

Inevitably, authors reflect the social and political preoccupations of their times, and authors of these texts of the 1970s reflect a society trying to end discrimination. Some key goals of the histories of the past have been dropped. For instance, from 1880 to 1920 histories taught abstract moral lessons. As the influential psychologist G. Stanley Hall wrote in 1911, "For school purposes, as for Carlyle, history should be to teach the infinite difference between good and bad, to set forth, even if in loud colors, the law of right and wrong, justice and injustice" (Hall, *Educational Problems*, II, Appleton, 1911, p. 290). We will find little of this today. And not one of the new histories claims as a principal objective inculcating patriotism, a function embraced by the history texts that appeared during and soon after World War I. Moralism and nationalism are both out of date.

The current texts, however, do maintain the view of progressive historians of the 1920s that the past should be studied in order to produce enlightened citizens—men and women who can critically analyze contemporary society and develop solutions to its problems (Tryon, *The Social Sciences as School Subjects,* Scribners, 1935, pp. 80-89). Like the old progressive histories, our texts try to develop in students an understanding of the past that is oriented to the solution of contemporary problems. The words of a leading progressive educator in 1916 would apply as well today: "Past events cannot be separated from the living present and retain meaning. The true starting point of history is always some present situation with its problems" (John Dewey, *Democracy and Education,* Macmillan, 1916, p. 250f.).

But one critical difference between the current texts and the progressive texts is in the treatment of ethnicity. The new histories treat ethnicity as a key element in historical analysis; an understanding of ethnicity is presented as indispensable for finding ways to improve present conditions. In the progressive histories, the ethnic pluralism of American society was typically seen as a divisive force impairing the integration of a democratic nation-state. Progressive history was shaped by a concern with revitalizing civic life and purifying politics. Current texts, in contrast, aim to improve society by expanding sympathy for different racial and ethnic groups.

Measuring the Treatment

How can we measure the salience of ethnic groups in the new textbooks? One rough gauge is a count of the number of pages devoted to major ethnic groups; another approach is to see what aspects of ethnic groups are emphasized. Table 1 shows the number of pages devoted to each group in each text.

In counting the number of pages devoted to American Indians, blacks, Mexicans, Puerto Ricans, Chinese, Japanese, "old [European] immigrants," and "new [European] immigrants," we followed no abstract logic but the actual patterns of the texts themselves. They have a great deal to say about American Indians and blacks. Because of the involvements of Mexicans, Puerto

TABLE 1

PAGES DEVOTED TO ETHNIC GROUPS
(Number and Percentage)

	BASS		LEINWAND		LINDEN		RISJORD		SHENTON		TODD	
Number of pages in text	776		726		768		842		768		784	
Indians	9.1	1.2%	9.3	1.3%	15.4	2.0%	21.0	2.5%	7.9	1.0%	11.7	1.5%
Blacks	37.0	4.8	47.5	6.5	20.3	2.6	37.4	4.4	24.5	3.2	33.4	4.3
Mexicans	1.0	0.1	1.8	0.2	0.3	0.04	2.1	0.2	0.8	0.1	1.3	0.2
Puerto Ricans	0.3	0.04	1.0	0.1	0.2	0.03	0.5	0.05	0.0	0.0	1.3	0.2
Chinese	0.7	0.1	0.4	0.1	0.6	0.1	0.6	0.07	0.3	0.04	1.1	0.1
Japanese	2.8	0.4	0.6	0.1	0.1	0.01	1.6	0.2	0.3	0.04	0.5	0.1
All Northern and Western Europeans	21.1	2.7	7.8	1.1	3.2	0.4	2.8	0.3	4.1	0.5	2.9	0.4
All Southern and Eastern Europeans	18.1	2.3	7.4	1.1	3.2	0.4	4.3	0.5	3.5	0.5	1.0	0.1
TOTAL	90.1	11.6%	75.8	10.4%	43.3	5.6%	70.3	8.3%	41.4	5.4%	53.2	6.8%

17

Ricans, Chinese, and Japanese in American wars and foreign policy disputes, the texts have occasional things to say about these groups. The treatment of immigrants from Europe, aside from occasional and passing mention of Irish, Germans, Scandinavians, Russians, Italians, and other groups, is primarily in terms of the classic distinction between immigrants from northwestern Europe (dominating American immigration until the 1880s) and immigrants from southern and eastern Europe (dominating American immigration after the 1890s).

Blacks, it is clear, receive the most attention: 47.5 pages in Leinwand, 37 in Risjord and Bass, 20 to 33 in other texts. American Indians are next with 21 pages in Risjord, 15 in Linden, and 8 to 12 in the others. In contrast, only a few pages—often not even one—are given to any discussion of Mexicans, Puerto Ricans, Chinese, and Japanese. One wonders whether this great disparity between the treatment of blacks and Indians and the treatment of Hispanics and Asians will survive the rapid increase in Hispanic, Korean, Filipino, and Southeast Asian immigrants, and the rise of bilingual and bicultural programs.

European immigrant groups receive only a fraction—in all but one history, a quarter or less—of the coverage given to non-whites and Hispanics. In part, this imbalance is due to the tendency of the texts to describe the populations of cities in the nineteenth and twentieth centuries in ethnically anonymous terms. The people are usually characterized under collective terms such as "industrial workers" or "immigrant city-dwellers"; their role is not hinged upon their ethnic origins or identification.

Differences in Ethnic Themes

There are also differences in the themes emphasized for different groups. For Indians it is their native culture and their warfare with whites; for blacks, slavery and its aftermath, continuing prejudice and discrimination, the efforts of reformers to improve the condition of blacks and the resultant creation of reform institutions and movements, and the recent adoption of new anti-discriminatory national policies; for European immigrants, the emphasis is on their role in urban and industrial development.

One topic of interest to sociologists, and increasingly to historians (Stephan Thernstrom, Josef Barton, and others), is the relation between ethnicity and social mobility. Do the texts treat this? Some introduce elementary concepts of social stratification and social mobility. However, the opportunities facing different ethnic groups and their success in capitalizing upon them are never probed. The new histories are shallow in considering how ethnic groups were integrated into the social system, and the crucial historical question of how well American society functioned, in actuality as well as in myth, as a land of opportunity for specific ethnic groups. Perhaps they fear that analysis would be tedious or would result in invidious group comparisons. Instead they tend to furnish biographical vignettes of the "rags to riches" variety, of individual successes meant to represent an ethnic group (Shenton, pp. 53-54).

The texts stress the frequency of "victimization" of ethnic minorities in American history. They usually attribute it to "tragic" circumstances—ignorance of other cultures, fear of strange appearance, prejudice, and unavoidable "culture clash" between a free-enterprise, industrializing society and populations with preindustrial forms of social and culture life. We have counted how many pages characterize ethnic groups as "victims" of prejudice or discrimination as against "beneficiaries" of reform ideas or programs. Post-colonial European immigrants are generally shown as "victims," rarely as "beneficiaries." Blacks are shown as "beneficiaries" of humanitarian concern and reform in almost as many pages as they are shown as "victims." The history of Indians is largely presented as a history of victimization. Mexicans, Puerto Ricans, Chinese, and Japanese too are characterized mainly as "victims"; they receive no treatment as "beneficiaries."

Ethnics in Pictures

Since the abundant illustrations of the new histories give a dramatic visual impression of the character of American history and of the roles of ethnic groups, we counted how many pictures portray ethnic group members (table 2). Our distribution is based on visual evidence in which it seems clear that the point of the

TABLE 2

PICTURES SHOWING ETHNIC GROUPS
(Number and Percentage)

	BASS		LEINWAND		LINDEN		RISJORD		SHENTON		TODD	
Number of pictures in text	401		346		347		319		361		374	
Indians	9	2.2%	15	4.3%	31	8.9%	18	5.6%	9	2.5%	20	5.3%
Blacks	33	8.2	58	16.8	51	14.7	24	7.5	35	9.7	49	13.1
Mexicans	2	0.5	1	0.3	11	3.2	1	0.3	5	1.4	2	0.5
Puerto Ricans	0	0.0	3	0.9	1	0.3	0	0.0	0	0.0	1	0.3
Chinese	4	1.0	2	0.6	8	2.3	3	0.9	1	0.2	1	0.3
Japanese	3	0.7	2	0.6	12	3.5	1	0.3	1	0.2	1	0.3
All Northern and Western Europeans	8	2.0	5	1.5	6	1.7	3	0.9	1	0.2	2	0.5
All Southern and Eastern Europeans	13	3.2	15	4.3	20	5.8	6	1.8	3	0.8	3	0.8
TOTAL	72	18.0%	101	29.2%	140	40.3%	56	17.6%	55	15.2%	79	21.1%

pictures is to present someone as identifiably from a specific ethnic group and on captions that specifically identify persons shown as members of an ethnic group. The percentage of pictures with persons identifiable or identified as being of an ethnic group ranged from a high of 40.3 in Linden to a low of 15.2 in Shenton. Blacks appeared in the greatest proportions: in 16.8 per cent of the pictures in Leinwand, 14.7 in Linden, and 13.1 in Todd. American Indians had the second greatest visual salience, followed by southern and eastern Europeans. Very few pictures showed Mexicans, Puerto Ricans, Chinese, and Japanese; the percentage of pictures containing Mexicans was no higher than 3.2 in any book, while in nearly every book less than 1 per cent of all pictures showed Puerto Ricans, Chinese, and Japanese.

The new texts give more coverage to ethnic groups than previous histories, but they have established a hierarchy of ethnic significance in American history. In the combined effect of text and pictures, blacks, Indians, and southern and eastern Europeans stand out. Much vaguer impressions are conveyed of northern and western Europeans, Hispanics, and Asian peoples, and their roles in the development of American society.

CHAPTER THREE

The Colonial Period And Before

TO CHARACTERIZE THE TREATMENT of ethnic groups is no simple matter, and no simple count will do. It is necessary to work through the texts, to see what information and judgments are presented, with what tone and feeling, for each group, and we have done so. We will try to characterize the various ethnic treatments by moving through the texts chronologically.

INDIANS

Those concerned for traditional history will be happy to learn that, while our texts do have a strong orientation to the present, they give substantial space to colonial history. In the beginning chapters we find extended discussions of the pre-Columbian Indian populations of the New World, their political organization, economy, and culture, and how they helped European colonists adapt to the conditions of the New World. Some of the texts refer to them as "the first Americans" (Todd, p. 10; Risjord, p. 2). Only one, Risjord, designates Indians as Native Americans with a capital *N*. (That book also capitalizes "Whites" and "Blacks.")

The discussions of Indian societies go back as much as 50,000 years, when the ancestors of American Indians crossed the Bering Strait from Asia to settle in the New World. We are told that they were divided into many different tribal societies, each with its own unique language and culture. The authors want to make sure the reader understands that American Indians are a diverse population of numerous ethnic groups. "There were some 600 different groups native to North America, speaking as many as 2,000 languages and dialects" (Bass, p. 57). "The American Indian speaks more than 500 languages in North America alone. Some of these were as different from each other as English is from Chinese. . . . Indian ways, customs, dress, tools, speech and foods varied greatly from tribe to tribe and region to region. Some Indians knew how to irrigate fields. . . . Some were very artistic and produced objects of great beauty. . . . Some built canals and floating gardens" (Leinwand, p. 4).

The texts report on crop-raising, material crafts, commerce, tribal government, religion, and social institutions in considerable detail, to show the creativity and autonomous innovation of Indian societies. "The development of Indian culture shows how simple societies can become increasingly complex even without interference or contact with other people" (Leinwand, p. 5).

Further, the texts suggest ways in which Indian society equaled or surpassed European. The Pueblos, for example, developed a society in which "there were no social classes or differences in wealth . . ." (Risjord, p. 8). The Indians are pictured as possessing a noble kind of communism that contrasted favorably with European property institutions: "Tribal ownership of land merely meant the right to use it. Indians were willing to share that use with others. But they simply could not accept the European idea of real estate as something fenced off for one's exclusive use" (Shenton, p. 22). Women held an "important position" in Indian society, serving as clan heads and owning "crops, as well as the houses and furniture" (Risjord, p. 8). By establishing a pluralistic system for making tribal decisions, Indians also originated the earliest "form of democratic government" in the New World (Linden, p. 24; Leinwand, p. 4). In certain Indian tribes, "democratic ways of making decisions sought a delicate balance between individual dignity and group interest" (Todd, p. 66).

The texts review the achievements of the Mayas, the Incas, and the Aztecs. "The Mayas built a brilliant civilization, carving great cities out of the jungles of Mexico. . . . Many years before the

Europeans arrived, the Mayas had a civilization equal to any in the world" (Risjord, p. 4). Linden notes that the Mayas' pyramids were "some of the world's great works in architecture" and that through astral time measurement the Mayas developed a calendar more accurate than what "was used in Europe at the time of Columbus" (Linden, p. 38). The Incas also come in for praise for their state-sponsored building projects, highly efficient irrigation system, and extensive road network for relay runners carrying messages to all corners of the empire (Linden, pp. 39-40; Leinwand, p. 5; Shenton, pp. 30-31).

The great Indian empires played no role in shaping the social development of the British North American colonies, of course; they are cited chiefly to inform the reader that the Indians of the New World were capable of developing high civilizations displaying sophisticated art and technology, complex social systems, and efficient forms of government.

What Indians Taught the Colonists

But other Indians did "contribute" many items to the stock of artifacts and skills that enabled European colonists to build up frontier societies. Europeans gained from them knowledge of half of the world's domesticated crops, among them corn, potatoes, cotton, tobacco, lima beans, and peanuts. They learned to extract cocaine, novocaine, and ephedrine from plants. Indians taught the Europeans how to clear the woodland, to make arable fields, trap and hunt game, and "fashion moccasins, snowshoes, and canoes" (Todd, pp. 27, 66; Leinwand, p. 7; Linden, p. 26; Shenton, p. 20). We are told that their influence over the growth of American society would have been even more positive if Europeans had accepted the Indians' subtle and respectful attitudes toward the environment, had learned to protect and conserve natural resources instead of exploiting them, and had taken more seriously the Indians' communal concept of ownership (Shenton, pp. 21-22; Leinwand, p. 7). What seems to matter to the authors is that students be prodded into thinking about the loss to American culture resulting from the Europeans' failure, through ignorance, prejudice, and fear, to appreciate Indian achievements. "In recent years," Todd asserts, "people everywhere have begun to relearn the priceless wisdom of the Indians' concern for living in harmony with nature and the land" (Todd, p. 67).

The encounter of Indians and Europeans and the subsequent destruction of the Indian societies is described in most of the texts as tragic but inevitable. "The saddest thing about the struggle between Indian and European settler was that it seemed impossible to avoid" (Shenton, p. 22).

Misunderstanding based on "culture clash" polarized the races. Neither side could understand the other's view of property or the natural environment. Treaties meant one thing to the colonists, another to the Indians. The Indians "neither understood nor cared" for the colonists' manufacturing and commerce, while Europeans could not fathom the Indians' refusal to embrace their ways. When war came, the colonists perceived the Indians' guerrilla tactics as proof "that the Indians were untrustworthy, cruel savages, and beyond the bounds of human civilization." Prejudice, fear, and the breakdown of communication divided the European from the Indian and established the conditions for "a long-lasting pattern of conflict" (Todd, pp. 68-69).

Despite the emphasis on the tragic, no question is left as to where the burden of moral culpability lies. In the strongest criticism of white settlers, "English greed" is given as the major cause of "mistrust and hostility," and atrocities committed by settlers against Indians are given greater prominence than the reverse. Quite typically, in the treatment of colonial wars, as later in the treatment of Indian warfare in the South and on the plains, massacres by whites are presented as massacres, massacres by Indians as an understandable response to loss of land and other wrongs. As Bass sums it up: "To Europeans the discovery of the New World meant opportunity. To the native peoples who had lived there for thousands of years it meant catastrophe. The coming of the Europeans brought death to millions of Indians and destroyed entire tribes" (p. 57).

The position of the Native American, in short, is presented with sympathy and understanding, and no little romanticization.

BLACKS

For blacks, too, a grim account of suffering is contrasted with glowing descriptions of the high civilizations blacks created in Africa: "Long before Europeans arrived in the New World, a number of African societies had reached a high degree of civilization. . . . [T]he ancient empire of Ghana . . . reached the peak of its power 500 years before Columbus sailed for America. Ghana's empire was held together by an efficient political system and a well-trained army" (Todd, p. 267). Timbuktu, a major city of the Kingdom of Mali, which replaced Ghana, possessed an eminent university that "became world renowned as a center of Islamic scholarship" (Risjord, p. 254). We are told, too, of the achievements of Dahomey, Benin, and Ashanti (Todd, pp. 267-68; Risjord, pp. 53, 253-55; Shenton, pp. 36-37). The "detailed ivory carving, ironwork, and bronze sculpture of Benin leave an eloquent record of its civilization. European accounts of the splendor of Benin describe streets as wide as those of Amsterdam, and a palace as large as a whole European city" (Risjord, p. 255). This European traveler (and others) probably engaged in hyperbole, but there is no hint of that in these texts, for their aim is to convince students that indigenous African culture, like American Indian culture, was a substantial human achievement that could have made a great contribution to American society.

When blacks began to lose their cultural heritage under slavery, says one text, whites were impoverished by the loss of African crafts and technical knowledge. "The white colonists ignored the skills already possessed by the black arrivals. Few white colonists knew or cared that the Africans came from civilizations hundreds or even thousands of years old. . . . Black newcomers were forced by their new circumstances to abandon most of what they had long cherished" (Todd, p. 61).

The terrible voyage by sea to the New World, the middle passage, is presented with all its horrors. "A slave ship that arrived with one half or even two thirds of its cargo dead was not unusual" (Risjord, p. 55). "A quarter of the human cargo regularly died in the overcrowded, disease-ridden ships" (Shenton, p. 39). Another text asserts that the loss of life was probably between 15 and 25 per cent (Bass, p. 64). Leinwand presents a particularly gruesome depiction of the middle passage:

> Once the ship left port escape seemed hopeless. The slaves then devised ways of killing themselves. Some, using only their nails, tore at their throats until they bled to death. Others starved themselves to death, despite the efforts of captains to feed them by force. Some jumped overboard during the exercise periods on deck. Still others "willed" themselves to death. These died of unknown causes. They seemed simply to lie down and die [Leinwand, p. 20].

The texts explain that social and economic conditions were the key factors stimulating the spread of slavery and the growth of popular racial prejudice. The expansion of commercial agriculture and the inefficiency of indentured servitude combined to produce an immense demand for slave labor. Pre-existing English ideas of the subhuman status of blacks assisted initial exploitation, but institutionalized racial slavery magnified these notions into an elaborated racial prejudice. "Once black men and women were enslaved, it was only a matter of time before whites began to think slavery was the natural condition of blacks" (Shenton, p. 39). The textbooks described the origins of slavery along the lines argued by Oscar and Mary Handlin in their famous article "Origins of the Southern Labor System" (*William and Mary Quarterly,* 1950): The status of blacks in early seventeenth-century society was similar to that of indentured servants. Slavery for blacks became an inherited condition. Because of slavery, blacks became popularly regarded as a permanently degraded people naturally suited for lifelong bondage (Bass, pp. 64-65; Todd, p. 21; Linden, p. 74; Risjord, pp. 55-56).

A draconian discipline, embodied in legal slave codes, was systematically imposed to suppress rebellion and to extract more labor. "A South Carolina law required overseers to whip any slave on their plantations who did not have proper identification. . . . The cruel treatment handed out by some owners was limited only by the master's imagination" (Bass, p. 67). "William Byrd of Virginia considered himself a kindly master. Yet about once a month he found it necessary to have some slave whipped, beaten or branded with a hot iron" (Shenton, p. 59).

Slaves, we are told, did not always passively submit. "We can only guess how slaves learned to hide their feelings at the mistreatment they received. . . . The number of slave rebellions and uprisings shows that they were sometimes unable to do so" (Shenton, p. 59). Blacks are pictured as active, willful agents, not as a submissive mass. Organized rebellions "came as early as the 1640's in Virginia, when slaves banded together with White servants in an unsuccessful uprising" (Risjord, p. 56). Blacks joined Indians in attacking a settlement at Hartford, Connecticut, in 1657; in 1712 "nine whites were killed during a slave uprising in New York City" (Shenton, p. 57). Boston slaves were accused of setting fire to the city in 1723, and in 1740 New York slaves "were charged with trying to poison the water supply" (Leinwand, p. 39). But "the most serious uprising took place in South Carolina in 1739. A band of nearly 100 slaves killed the Whites in their vicinity. . ." (Risjord, p. 56).

The most "common form of resistance," we are told, was "running away" (Risjord, p. 56), or sabotage. "Whenever possible, they purposely slowed down their work or did it poorly" (Todd, p. 63).

The treatment of slaves was hardly better in the North than in the South, the texts assert. "New England slaves, like slaves everywhere, rebelled against the central evil of slavery. . . . Many New England slaves fled from their masters, no matter how kind their masters might be" (Todd, p. 62). Yet the texts observe that the slave's life in New England and the middle colonies offered opportunities to obtain education and to enter into skilled trades (Leinwand, p. 39; Todd, p. 62; Shenton, p. 57).

The Plight of Free Blacks

We also find portrayals of the difficult lives of free blacks: "[T]hey held low-paying jobs as house servants, dock workers, and sailors," and "for most of them life was little different than it was for slaves" (Bass, p. 68). Todd, however, contradicts this view, observing that most free blacks worked as craftsmen, farmers, and small proprietors, and that some even won a "respected place in their communities" (p. 64). All the histories agree that free blacks in every colony lived in the shadow of discriminatory laws and customs: "Blacks were routinely separated in Church. . . . They were buried in separate parts of the graveyard. . . . Occasionally, one or two Black children attended school with white children" (Risjord, p. 57). "They often could not join the colonial militia, could not vote, and often could not testify in court against whites" (Bass, p. 68). Those who were "merchants or artisans often had a hard time getting customers" (Leinwand, p. 39). "In the 1700's free Negroes were not allowed to vote in any of the Southern Colonies except, for a time, in North Carolina" (Todd, p. 64).

Thus no student today should be ignorant of the fact that in colonial society blacks were condemned to servile labor and subjected to a blanket of discriminatory laws and customs. Widespread racial prejudice buttressed the stone wall of unequal and exploitative treatment. Two points stand out vividly: the great suffering endured by blacks, and their continuous resistance to enslavement and discrimination.

Black Contributions

Yet despite the barriers "Black men and women contributed significantly to the life of the colonies" (Risjord, p. 58). Benjamin Banneker is described as a "mechanical genius" who "published an *almanac* that was almost as widely known as Benjamin Franklin's" (Risjord, p. 58). Phillis Wheatley, a poet, produced "probably the most distinctive literature in colonial America . . ." (Leinwand, p. 43). Crispus Attucks, a sailor, is portrayed as "the first casualty of the American Revolution" (Risjord, p. 86), and Peter Salem is shown killing a British officer, Major Pitcairn, at the Battle of Bunker Hill (Leinwand, p. 71). "[T]here was hardly a major battle in which there were no blacks" (Leinwand, p. 71). "In all, some 5,000 black Americans served in the Continental navy and armies and in the navies and militias of the states" (Todd, p. 119).

Blacks are shown to have had some white defenders. As early as 1700, Samuel Sewall, "a legislator and judge in Massachusetts

Bay," published *The Selling of Joseph,* which "spoke out against slavery" (Risjord, p. 57). Eventually, Quakers and Moravians outlawed the possession of slaves in their communities (Risjord, p. 57). "John Woolman, a conscientious and thoughtful Quaker tailor, journeyed through the colonies trying to persuade Quakers to free their slaves and educate them" (Todd, p. 64). After the American Revolution, abolitionist societies sprouted in the northern colonies (Todd, p. 125); when these colonies became states they proceeded to outlaw slavery.

The Constitution takes up a large space in each of the texts. All describe it as a product of wise statecraft that endured because of its flexibility and its system of delicate balances and separation of powers, but all emphasize the failure to end the slave trade immediately and to eradicate slavery in all the states. The founders, we are told, feared that "an attack on slavery would make it difficult to get the Constitution ratified. Others feared that to attack one form of property would lead to attacks on other forms. Few believed that if the slaves were freed, blacks and whites could live together in a just and peaceful society" (Shenton, p. 110). Practical statecraft necessitated a painful, troubling compromise on this issue: "The slave trade compromise was probably necesary for the Constitution to gain needed support in the South. At the time the Constitution was written, many Americans believed that slavery was gradually dying out and this would no longer be a problem . . ." (Todd, p. 141). "At best, the compromise was a product of the time. At worst, it planted the virus that infected the body of the Union" (Leinwand, p. 86). Because of the compromise "the most dangerous of issues had only been postponed" (Shenton, p. 110), and Todd writes that as a result "a tragic war would finally bring an end to slavery in the United States" (Todd, p. 141). The texts teach us that the Constitution abandoned blacks to the demands of political realism.

EUROPEAN IMMIGRANTS

For European immigrants, the colonies are pictured as beacons of freedom, toleration, and economic opportunity (Linden, p. 68) that attracted thousands of non-English peoples. In the seventeenth century, Rhode Island's "climate of freedom attracted new immigrants, among them Jews" (Risjord, p. 37). When William Penn promised "complete religious freedom" in his new colony of Pennsylvania, persecuted German pietists and Scotch-Irish streamed in (Risjord, pp. 43-44; Shenton, p. 49); Swiss newcomers and "Jews from many countries of Europe" flocked to Pennsylvania (Todd, p. 35). Seeking religious asylum, thousands of French Huguenots settled in New York; "an even larger group . . . went to Charleston, South Carolina" (Shenton, p. 52; Todd, p. 37). "There in 1703, Jews voted in a general election for the first time in the western world. Furthermore, they were allowed to enter any profession they wished—a freedom denied both Jews and non-Jews in other colonies" (Risjord, pp. 61-62).

Still, we are informed that many immigrants did not find complete religious liberty or toleration after arrival: "The Jews, and to a greater extent the Catholics, continued to suffer discrimination throughout colonial times" (Linden, p. 79). "Neither Catholics nor Jews enjoyed full political freedom" (Leinwand, p. 127). Risjord observes that Jews found "Puritan Massachusetts, Anglican Virginia, and Roman Catholic Maryland" so inhospitable that "no Jewish communities of any size developed there" (Risjord, p. 62). Gradually, however, "the spirit of religious toleration began to grow" (Todd, p. 72), and "religious liberty was slowly won" (Leinwand, p. 127); as Todd points out, the presence of a variety of religious groups and the labor needs of the colonies were strong pressures promoting toleration (Todd, p. 78).

Economic Opportunities for Immigrants

The texts agree that the British colonies furnished economic opportunity beyond that provided by any European nation or dominion. Shenton calls the colonies "the best poor man's country," for "from the beginning colonial society had no fixed class structure" (Shenton, p. 53). "Through hard work and ability an artisan or even a white servant could make a fortune and join the society of the influential townspeople and southern planters" (Todd, p. 54). Most male immigrants became middling farmers, tradesmen, or proprietors and received the franchise, a privilege unattainable in their European homelands. Even if some could not rise from poverty, they did not suffer starvation and destitution as did many peasants in Europe. And some newcomers achieved spectacular and rapid success: "Robert Buchanan, a Scotsman, came to America in 1760 as an apprentice. Six years later he was a partner in a large business. Bernard Corey, an Irish cloth dealer, arrived in 1766 with a little money. In ten years he owned 6,000 acres of land and a large herd of livestock" (Shenton, pp. 53-55).

The texts emphasize the variety of customs and culture brought by immigrants to colonial society. The newcomers "added color and variety to the colonial population" (Shenton, p. 52). Todd takes the reader on an imaginary stroll through mid-eighteenth-century Philadelphia. "On the streets . . . you hear the accents of people from France, Switzerland, Sweden, and many other European countries." And with a degree of specificity not common in these texts, Todd goes on to record the new words from the Indian, Dutch, and French languages, and also the totally new creations, that by the 1760s had entered English and led Samuel Johnson to refer to the English of the colonies as the "American dialect" (Todd, p. 56).

Thus students should learn that the British colonies probably offered the widest economic opportunities and religious liberties available in any society at the time. But they also learn that colonial expansion led to the destruction of Indian cultures, the reduction of Indian population, and the mass enslavement of blacks, and that European domination resulted in the legal and customary treatment of blacks and Indians as inferior beings.

CHAPTER FOUR

The Expanding New Nation

SOON AFTER THE CONSOLIDATION of the federal government, we enter a period characterized by the pushing back of the frontier, territorial expansion, new wars, and rapid economic growth. Indians continue to play a leading role in the story.

INDIANS

Simple land hunger, we are told, was the primary cause of the destruction of the Indian tribes. Skirmishes with Indians in the Old Northwest began after 1800 because of "the settlers' greed for Indian land in the West." From 1800 to 1810, Indian tribes were "driven off 100 million acres" in the Ohio Valley "through force or through trickery" (Bass, p. 228). The War Hawks were "eager to increase westward migration"; since the "biggest obstacle to that was the Indians . . . a major confrontation with them was shaping up" (Shenton, p. 156). To resist the encroachment of white settlers, Tecumseh, a "brilliant" Shawnee leader, organized a league of tribes from Canada to the Gulf Coast that impeded movement into the Old Northwest. He fought William Henry Harrison, the governor of the Indiana Territory, who used "every possible means—bribery, liquor, threats" to "further Indian land cessions" (Risjord, p. 204). "Time after time, the Indians had been promised that this was the last land they would be forced to give up. And every time the promise had been broken" (Todd, p. 209).

Only one history text reminds the reader that officially Indian tribes were outside American civil society and that the U.S. government, as well as the Indians themselves, regarded Indian tribes as separate, sovereign nations with ambiguous relationships to the United States. This fact would not excuse the shabby treatment of the Indians, but it does help to clarify why the federal government dealt warily and duplicitously with the tribes, who were often seen as potentially hostile foreign nations and allies of foreign nations. By failing to discuss this problem, the texts reduce the complex, tangled relations among white settlers, Indians, and the federal government to a simple phenomenon caused by pure American greed.

Removal of the 'Civilized Tribes'

Every text supplies an extensive account of the removal of the Five Civilized Tribes from Georgia, Florida, Alabama, and Mississippi under the administration of Andrew Jackson. Ironically, the ascent of Andrew Jackson to the presidency, which signified the spread of popular democracy to whites, resulted in perhaps the most massive violation of Indian rights in the nation's history. The Creeks, Choctaws, Chickasaws, Cherokees, and Seminoles, once powerful tribes, had "adopted many of the white settlers' ways of life" (Todd, p. 239). Cultivating European crops with European farming methods and converted to Christianity, these tribes were secured in their status and rights by federal treaties, one signed by Andrew Jackson himself (Shenton, p. 192). The Cherokees had created their own "written constitution" providing for "a legislature, a judicial system, and a law enforcing militia" (Todd, p. 239). "They had their own written language, and some of the wealthy farmers owned black slaves, as their white neighbors did" (Linden, p. 162). But as "land-hungry" whites moved in, they pressured the state and the federal government to rescind the treaties.

This led to the destruction of the civilized Indian nations and the forced removal of the tribes to Oklahoma. The resolute Cherokees obtained a U.S. Supreme Court decision declaring unconstitutional certain removal laws passed by the Georgia legislature. As Leinwand tells us, President Jackson retorted, "John Marshall has made his decision; now let him enforce it" (Leinwand, p. 174). Jackson sent soldiers, who "rousted the Cherokees from their homes" (Risjord, p. 276), and the Indians "were marched at bayonet point to what today we would call concentration camps" (Leinwand, p. 175). Leinwand quotes Peter Farb's *Man's Rise to Civilization* (New York, 1968, p. 253) to compare the removal of the Cherokees to the Nazi incarceration of the Jews: "They were torn from their homes with all the dispatch and efficiency the Nazis displayed under similar circumstances" (Leinwand, p. 175). There follows in each text the terrible forced march to the West along "the trail of tears."

How do the new histories explain why Jackson, the exponent of egalitarian democracy, endorsed such grossly unjust and illegal treatment? Todd resolves this apparent contradiction by indicating that Jackson was a product of his times, and that American ideas of equality and justice did not yet apply for Indians, blacks, women, criminals, the mentally ill, or, for that matter, even workers. Jackson, "by the standards of the times, took important strides toward fuller political democracy" (Todd, pp. 239-40). All true enough; and yet one wonders whether the 1979 frame of understanding of just who deserve equal rights (one notes that the handicapped and aged have been left out of Todd's catalog) need be applied so literally and mechanically to explain Jackson's treatment of the Indians.

The fate of the Indians as the frontier moves west remains a major focus of attention. Occasional Indian military victories are seen as heroic acts of resistance, "an effort to hold on to their lands and to keep their distinctive ways of life" (Todd, p. 394; Risjord, pp. 420-22; Bass, pp. 486-90; Shenton, pp. 345-49; Linden, pp. 301-3), while the killing of Indians by the Army is often described as massacre (Leinwand, p. 314; Risjord, p. 422; Shenton, p. 348). From the accounts given, the alert student can deduce that Indians were engaged in massacre as well as whites. But the contrast of white massacre and Indian resistance, of brilliant Indian chiefs and executioner white generals, reveals the tendency in the current histories—despite attention to the tragic aspects of the encounter of two such disparate societies—to slip into a crude dualism of good and evil, one that simply reverses the roles held by whites and Indians in earlier texts.

The attempt to acculturate and to assimilate the Indian, whether on the reservation or off, is pictured in some of the texts as brutal. Shenton calls the Dawes Act (offering land and citizenship to Indians who gave up tribal connection) "another way of stealing land," since speculators took advantage of loopholes within it to acquire "two thirds of the reservation lands" held by tribes in 1887 (Shenton, p. 349). Todd (p. 396) and Risjord (pp. 425-26) tell the same story.

The reservation system is described critically. Indian children in reservation schools "were taught, often by poorly trained and unsympathetic teachers, to look down on Indian ways of life as inferior and degraded" (Todd, p. 396). "[I]nsensitive bureaucrats in Washington ordered that henceforth Indian men must cut their hair short. . . . Like Samson in the Bible they felt that long hair protected them from harm. Federal troops had to be sent to carry out the order. Held in chains, the Indians were shorn like lambs" (Leinwand, p. 318).

The late nineteenth century was "the Indians' darkest period. . . . Yet their vitality and spirit were reflected even then in the continuing demand by many of them that they be regarded as separate, self-respecting peoples with worthy ways of viewing human relationships, of understanding their part in the environment, and of sensing their place in the universe" (Todd, p. 396). And yet one would suspect that Indian traditional cultures survived, in some measure, not only because Indians believed them superior, but also because under the reservation system Indians still possessed a measure of autonomy, and customs were too deeply rooted in centuries of practice and belief to be eliminated by an external and unsympathetic authority. One does not find such an interpretation discussed, for the writers of these texts want to stress the heroism and integrity of the Indians in the face of an overwhelming power.

BLACKS

The institution of slavery shaped the lives of blacks, was the cause of the great Civil War, and established enduring patterns of custom affecting subsequent social interaction between blacks and whites.

It has stimulated a vast outpouring of recent scholarship and interpretation. It is a severe test for these texts.

We note, to begin with, that they describe the population of blacks in bondage during the nineteenth century as "communities," "societies," and "cultures." They emphasize the autonomy, individuality, and separateness of black life even when blacks were daily exposed to the values and behavior of white masters and overseers. While some may argue with our use of the term "ethnic" to cover black as well as white groups, current texts, interestingly enough, do present the enslaved blacks as an ethnic group with a self-conscious identity and culture.

Most caution the reader about the difficulty of understanding slavery from the vantage point of the present. The discussion of slavery is one of the few points at which the texts pause to consider different historical interpretations and to indicate the inherent limits of historical reconstruction. "On the basis of documents and records alone, no historian can accurately reconstruct what it was like to be a slave. There are many records, but most of them were written by white southerners or by white travelers from the North" (Todd, p. 273).

The new histories portray the treatment of slaves as a mix of exploitation with paternalism and the economic imperative to keep healthy, productive workhands. "Since there was no control of a master's use of force, it is not surprising that angry and brutal masters often did real harm to the helpless slaves. Whipping was routinely used . . . " (Bass, p. 317). "When persuasion failed, masters and overseers could and did resort to brutality. . . . [S]laves . . . might be flogged or whipped . . . branded . . . or hav[e] their noses slit" (Todd, pp. 274-75).

But the physical abuse of slaves was usually checked because the injury or death "of a single slave meant a serious financial loss" (Todd, p. 274). "A master would indeed be very unwise not to take care of a field hand, who by the 1850's cost $1,700 to replace" (Bass, p. 316). Shenton tells us that "when dangerous work was to be done, planters often hired white laborers rather than risk their valuable property. A northern visitor once asked a Louisiana planter why some Irish workers were being used to drain a swamp.

He was quickly told that there was malaria in the swamp and that it was too unhealthy for slaves" (Shenton, p. 243). And the texts hold that slaves generally lived at about the same material level as factory hands in the North. They thus present a picture of slavery that lies midway between the pro-slavery argument that blacks received benevolent treatment and the abolitionist view that slave life was characterized by beatings, starvation, overwork, and death.

The Skills of Slaves

They try to counter any notion that slaves were defective in skill or intelligence, attacking the invidious idea "that slaves were inefficient, unskillful, and unable to learn new tasks quickly or easily" (Shenton, p. 242). They stress that many slaves were highly skilled and hard-working because of African custom: "The culture of the Ashanti and the Fantis of the Gold Coast, the Yorubas of Nigeria, and the Mandingos and Hausas of the Sudan had all developed a complex way of life. These were not people leading a simple, primitive existence. They were able, skilled, and hardworking farmers and craftsmen. These were precisely the qualities whites saw in them when they were first brought to these shores" (Leinwand, p. 202). "Men became blacksmiths, painters, shoemakers, jewelers, and silversmiths" (Todd, pp. 273-74); many slaves were "deckhands and firemen on Mississippi riverboats" and skilled mechanics (Leinwand, p. 207). Others learned the skills of building houses: "Some could not only build the house, but could also make necessary plans, draw up contracts, and complete the entire structure" (Todd, p. 274).

The emphasis on these skills is balanced by the argument that any evidence of low productivity could be explained by the slaves' purposeful efforts to resist the oppressive demands of masters by sabotage or uncooperativeness. "They might damage tools, steal, or work slowly or carelessly. What slaveowners took as lazy, clumsy behavior was for many slaves a way of resisting his or her condition" (Linden, p. 192). Bass describes "resistance" by slaves who "went so far as to cut off a hand or foot so that they could not do field work. Masters were never sure whether the slaves had

ing, sympathy, and respect for all groups. But they seem overzealous and unsteady in their approach. An overemphasis on racism and discrimination obscures the laudable social and economic achievements of American society.

It is true, regrettably, that Americans imported and enslaved blacks and even after slavery subjected them to segregation and discrimination; that until relatively recently they treated Indians cruelly and passed laws penalizing Chinese and Japanese; that they subjected Jews to anti-Semitism; and the like. Textbooks must tell this story.

But it is equally true that this country has accepted more immigrants, of more varied stocks, than any other nation in the world, and continues to do so; that it has been a beacon for immigrants, despite their knowledge of the prejudiced attitudes and the official discrimination they would find here; that it presents the world with the most successful example of a complex, modern, multi-ethnic society; and that it goes further than any other great country in creating a partnership of varied peoples, all of whom are guaranteed a range of rights and offered full participation in the common life of the nation.

Ethnic Groups in History Textbooks
By Nathan Glazer and Reed Ueda
80 pages   April 1983
Paper $4   ISBN 0-89633-064-8
Includes name index

Ethics and Public Policy Center
1030 Fifteenth Street N.W.
Washington, D.C. 20005
(202) 682-1200

Doing Justice to Diversity

A greater attention to the European ethnic groups would help the texts present a more complex, and truer, picture of American diversity, and of the problems and successes of the American political system in dealing with it. And such attention would indicate to students where *they* might fit into the story of the American people—something that a radical disjunction between "racist whites" and "victimized non-white minorities" does not readily permit for many students. The European ethnic groups offer a bridge of varied experiences between those of early and dominant white settlers and those of non-white victims—native, imported, or free immigrants. In providing such a bridge of experiences, they also indicate a potential course for those non-white minorities and new immigrants—increasingly non-white—who may still range below the mean in education, income, and influence.

Ultimately, when textbooks portray the history of ethnic groups as a repeated struggle between victims and oppressors—between subject and dominant peoples—the central processes that integrated American society are trivialized. For example, the student receives no sense of the impact of public schooling on the social and economic mobility of ethnic groups, of the relation of black migration to public efforts to combat discrimination, or of the role of immigrants in broadening American religious institutions. In concentrating narrowly on ethnic conflict, the new history slights the forces that have created common bases of group experience and group interests that transcend ethnic lines.

It is hard to believe that such one-sided approaches will do much to engage students. They live in a world in which school busing is an ever-present reality and affirmative action affects almost every civil servant and employee of a major organization; a world in which Democrats and Republicans alike eschew harsh and punitive measures in dealing with illegal immigration; a world in which they see Asian schoolmates advancing and new Asian immigrants beginning to progress through the cycles of past immigrants. What will they then make of histories that speak only of victims and exploiters in dealing with racial and ethnic minorities? Students can approach such histories only, one feels, with skepticism and incomprehension—or, if they put aside their living experience, they can only fall victim to misleading ideologies.

A Successful Multi-Ethnic Society

The writers of the textbooks examined in this study properly seek to engage the student's conscience in the process of creating a society that provides social justice for all ethnic groups. Thus they undermine complacency and try to replace it with an understand-

ethnic groups become major threads of the narrative. The expansion of the American nation to the West becomes the tragedy of the Indian. The history of the South becomes the story of slavery. The story of the growth of industry focuses on the suffering of immigrants. Despite this somewhat diffused focus, however, the familiar major outlines of American historical development are not ignored in the new texts, though they are somewhat reduced.

Glazer and Ueda measured the proportion of space devoted to ethnic groups in the texts. They found a range of 5.4 to 11.6 per cent, which they do not consider excessive. The problem was not in the amount of coverage but in its overall tone. The old myths of racial inferiority implicit in American texts of the twenties and thirties have been replaced by new myths proclaiming the superior moral qualities of minorities. In a kind of Manichaean inversion, whites are portrayed as malevolent and blacks, Indians, Asians, and Hispanics as tragic victims. The texts emphasize discrimination, prejudice, and victimization of selected minorities.

A New Civic Morality

The new histories foster a new civic morality whose major ingredients are an understanding of and respect for the humanity of disadvantaged minorities. By describing the social and cultural history of ethnic groups, the texts supply what might be called a basic level of "ethnic literacy." But it is very basic indeed. It emphasizes the positive features of each group, and elicits sympathy by vividly picturing the efforts of ethnic minorities to defend themselves from discrimination and to advance under inhospitable circumstances. Inevitably, this emphasis on discrimination and prejudice and on the struggle against oppression reduces the stature of the "white" majority, still the main protagonist of these histories.

The new texts have as yet found no way of incorporating any sophisticated or complex view of the white European immigrants of the nineteenth and twentieth centuries. This lack inevitably sharpens the disjunction between oppressors and oppressed, and tends on occasion to reduce American history to only that.

There is indeed a tale of oppressors and oppressed, and it must be told. But the white "oppressors" themselves form a complex mix of European ethnic groups, divided by language and religion. Many of these groups, too, have been victims of American nativism and the religious prejudices of the dominant Protestants. Yet without surrendering their identity or changing their religion they have become incorporated into the "white" majority. Almost all of them have achieved better education, higher incomes, jobs of higher status, and participation in the common political life of the United States. This is increasingly the experience of non-white groups also.

SUMMARY

Ethnic Groups in History Textbooks
By Nathan Glazer and Reed Ueda

O ne element of the American civil rights movement that came to the fore in the 1970s was a strong assertion of racial pride within the country's largest racial minority, the blacks. A similar development occurred among other ethnic groups that had been subjected to prejudice and discrimination, notably American Indians and Hispanics.

In response to this new consciousness, textbook publishers sought to correct the neglect of these ethnic minorities in history textbooks used in American high schools. The question subsequently arose: Was their reaction too extreme? Was the story of blacks, Indians, Asians, Hispanics, and other ethnic groups now exaggerated? Was there now too much emphasis on their tribulations? Was the role of the "white" majority too severely condemned? And, in refocusing the historical camera, did the textbook authors and editors lose sight of the central, unifying themes of our national history?

Nathan Glazer, professor of education and sociology at Harvard University, and Reed Ueda, assistant professor of history at Tufts University, examined these questions through an analysis of six American history high school texts from major textbook publishers.* They found that the new treatment of ethnicity changes a text from one with a single and simple national perspective to one that incorporates a variety of group perspectives. History can no longer be written from a single national point of view when the histories of

---

*The six texts are *Our American Heritage* by Herbert J. Bass and others (Silver Burdett, 1979); *The Pageant of American History* by Gerald Leinwand (Allyn and Bacon, 1975); *A History of Our American Republic* by Glenn M. Linden and others (Laidlaw Brothers [A Division of Doubleday], 1979); *People and Our Country* by Norman K. Risjord and Terry L. Haywoode (Holt, Rinehart and Winston, 1978); *These United States* by James P. Shenton and others (Houghton Mifflin, 1978); and *Rise of the American Nation* by Lewis Paul Todd and Merle Curti (Harcourt, Brace, Jovanovich, 1977).

planned these things or whether they occurred by sheer accident." He tells of a Louisiana physician who theorized that this form of behavior was caused by an organic malady found among Negroes known as "dyaesthesic aethioptica" (Bass, p. 319).

Two themes emphasized in the description of slave society and culture are the solidarity of black family life and the survival of African customs and traditions. We see reflected in these themes the work of such recent reinterpreters of slavery as Robert Fogel and Stanley Engermann, John Blassingame, and Herbert Gutman. While the reader is told of the cruel disruption of the families through the sale of members, the texts emphasize that black family life survived, and that family bonds were strong and vital. *"The heart of the slave community was the family"* (Risjord, p. 257 — italics and bold face). Although "[p]robably between 15 and 30 percent of the slave couples were separated by the sale of one of the mates, . . . many slaves were able to make family life work" (Bass, pp. 317-18).

Similarly, another source of autonomy in slave life is to be found in a culture welling up from deep African sources. "For a long time it was thought that the slaves' African culture simply disappeared after they landed in America. However, as we have learned more about African society, we have learned that a considerable amount of African culture did survive. For example, in many African societies when farming was done in groups, one person sang to set a rhythm for the others to work by. This practice was carried over into the tobacco, rice, and cotton fields of the American South" (Bass, p. 314). "Their ways of life included survivals of their African heritage combined with some traits of white southern culture. . . . Their hymns . . . were modeled in part on the 'gospel hymns' sung by white Christians, but they were also influenced by traditional African musical forms" (Todd, p. 276).

In some contradiction to his description of the survival of African work habits and skills, Leinwand asserts that the slave's "name, his tribe, his family, his history, his traditions, his religion and his customs were all 'blotted out' — that is, destroyed" (Leinwand, p. 204). Todd argues that the system of slave discipline infantilized a number of slaves, reflecting Stanley Elkins in his controversial work *Slavery: A Problem in American Institutional and Intellectual Life* (Chicago, 1959), which compared the psychological effects of slavery upon blacks to the damage suffered by inmates of Nazi concentration camps (Todd, p. 274). This view of the effects of slavery on the black personality, once popular among academic historians, is now considered highly dubious. That this idea should be retained in a 1977 textbook after the research of the last decade may reflect the author's considered judgment that Elkins is still right, but more likely it either is a residue from previous editions of the textbook that slipped past editorial scrutiny or reflects the author's failure to keep up with recent research and interpretation.

Runaways and Rebellions

All the texts devote substantial space to runaways and slave rebellions, which they regard as the most compelling evidence of the dissatisfaction of slaves and their desire for freedom. The texts also deal rather fully with the free blacks who campaigned against slavery. They strive to show a substantial degree of black autonomy in action even under slavery: "Free black Americans were deeply involved in the struggle to end slavery. In fact, a free black named David Walker published an abolitionist pamphlet in Boston in 1829, two years before Garrison's first issue of *The Liberator*" (Bass, p. 326). "Two of the most powerful speakers for the abolitionist cause were Frederick Douglass and Sojourner Truth" (Linden, p. 185). Blacks are shown as especially effective in running the Underground Railroad. "The most successful conductor on the Underground Railroad was Harriet Tubman. She herself was an ex-slave. She is credited with conducting 300 slaves to freedom" (Leinwand, pp. 193-94). "She was often called 'the Moses of her people,'" we read in a caption under her picture (Todd, p. 305).

One theme that emerges is that black reformers had to resist the assumption of authority by white colleagues. "[M]any black abolitionists found it difficult to work with the white-dominated antislavery movement. They charged they were never given positions of leadership. White abolitionists expected them to be work-

ers and speakers but seldom took their advice on important matters" (Shenton, p. 253). Black abolitionists like Frederick Douglass and Henry H. Garnet, we are told, preserved an independent
position criticizing white abolitionists who gave them advice about
how to behave (Bass, p. 327). We are meant to see black reformers
as independent figures, participating in the anti-slavery movement
with whites but not surrendering their individuality or their initia-
tive. Indeed, they are pictured as indispensable tutors to whites on
the experience of racial injustice and the proper relations of blacks
and whites.

With the end of slavery after the Civil War, the texts show the
newly freed blacks as a major force moving Southern political and
civic institutions closer to racial equality. The free blacks are
pictured as bravely trying to secure the full rights and privileges of
citizenship in the face of repressive black codes, Ku Klux Klan
assaults, and desultory support from the federal government.

"A body of skilled and educated blacks provided leadership" for
the newly freed slaves. "Many of them came from the blacks who
had lived in the South before the war; some were former slaves;
others came to the South as soldiers, Freedmen's Bureau agents, or
missionaries" (Shenton, p. 336). Through voting, office-holding,
and self-education they worked in the late 1860s and 1870s to
produce what "came to be called *Black Reconstruction,* a phrase
that seemed to say that blacks ruled the Southern states" (Bass, p.
368). But blacks, we are told, were never politically dominant.

The new histories attack historical interpretations of Reconstruction as a period of "black misrule." They insist that blacks
supported generally progressive changes. They did not support the
Republicans because of crude pay-offs: "[T]hey supported the
Republican Party for the sound reason that the Republicans were
more likely than the Democrats to supply [their] needs" (Shenton,
p. 336). We are told that the charge of "black misrule" was a smear
by the displaced whites, and that when compared to politics at the
federal level and in Northern states, political corruption in the
South was not excessive.

If Southern state budgets rose, it was not because of corruption
but because "most of the tax money went for new programs that

were designed to help the people" (Linden, p. 268). The new state governments in which blacks participated financed the expansion of free public schools, welfare programs for the needy, and a reorganization of judicial and prison systems (Todd, pp. 368-69; Linden, p. 268). Black politicians worked effectively with whites in achieving these reforms (Leinwand, p. 286). When they acted to advance the interests of blacks, black politicians concentrated on education, protecting the right to vote, and protecting black people against violence (Bass, p. 280).

The texts present the traditional account of the collapse of Reconstruction and the fashioning of the Southern system of segregation and caste oppression. One interesting test case of their responsiveness to new winds in black historiography is the treatment of Booker T. Washington. With the exception of one text, Washington is pictured not as a lackey of white industrialists and Southern planters but as a shrewd statesman with a patient plan for exploiting the limited opportunities available to blacks. Washington is criticized for accepting accommodation to Jim Crow, but the texts all show conditions so regressive that his compromise appears politic. Thus, after reporting the criticism of Washington for willingness to compromise black rights, Bass goes on: "Of late, however, historians have suggested that perhaps Washington was a smart politician who understood how to take the first step toward equality as preparation for the second. Often overlooked is the fact that Washington made clear that once blacks, as productive citizens, 'proved themselves worthy,' other steps toward equality must follow" (Bass, p. 388).

MEXICANS AND ASIANS

In the nineteenth-century sections of the new histories, the first discussions of Mexicans and Asian Americans appear. The amount of space devoted to these groups, especially the latter, is only a tiny fraction of that treating blacks and Indians. But the histories of Hispanics and Asians, like those of blacks and Indians, emphasize both their subjection to various forms of discrimination and exploitation and their positive qualities, which made no impression on contemporary Americans.

The texts describe the Mexicans who became part of the United States through annexation as a mixed group of Spanish, Indian, and Negro stock who possessed customs and a religion "that English-speaking Americans did not understand" (Risjord, p. 288). Antedating "the first settlers . . . to Jamestown or the Pilgrims to Plymouth," the Mexicans shaped much of the "character" of "the great American Southwest" (Leinwand, p. 232). The American cowboy learned the "techniques used by the Mexicans" to raise and to herd cattle (Risjord, pp. 432-33; Leinwand, p. 233). This rich "heritage of language, tradition, and religion" (Linden, p. 289) was regarded by "English-speaking Americans in the area . . . as inferior to their own" (Todd, p. 289). Because of this failure of understanding, "as the area was settled, conflicts would arise and adjustments would be made" (Risjord, p. 288).

White settlers, "Anglos," began to secure land titles from the Mexicans through purchase, intimidation, and questionable legal maneuvers. "By the Treaty of Guadalupe Hidalgo . . . and the Gadsden Purchase . . . property rights of Mexican Americans were supposed to be respected. . . . But often Anglo settlers were able to get the Mexican land deeds set aside" (Shenton, p. 351). After "the American takeover," Mexicans "worked for low wages on American ranches, in mines, or building railroads" (Todd, p. 289). The Mexicans sought better education and training, but "they continued to face job discrimination and to be among the first fired, last hired" (Linden, p. 210). Todd describes a severe culture conflict: "Their new employers looked down on them as lazy, superstitious, and inefficient. They, in turn, regarded the Americans as arrogant and domineering, in contrast with their own traditions of family loyalty, personal honor, devout Catholicism, and a noncompetitive way of life" (Todd, p. 289). The Mexicans come off as more attractive than their employers. Todd also portrays Mexican bandits as protestors "at least in part . . . against the injustices suffered by the peons. In response, . . . Texas and New Mexico Rangers were organized to enforce law and order but often resorted to brutal racial injustice, beatings, and lynchings" (Todd, p. 289). Once again one wonders whether a crude dualism—in this case, pernicious Anglos and exploited Mexicans—gives the right balance to history.

The Chinese appear for the first time in the new histories as pioneering newcomers who sought opportunities in mining, agriculture, and construction. They are also pictured as "the first victims of rising distrust against all immigrants" (Todd, pp. 442-43; Risjord, p. 462) and the first immigrant people to suffer sustained racist attacks. Although China had "a long and glorious history" and its people, "thrifty, hard-working, and law-abiding," could be expected to make "model citizens," "Americans preferred to see the Chinese as 'a degraded race, ignorant of civilized life,' as one magazine put it" (Shenton, p. 377). Subjected to racist hostility and discrimination, "they were often the victims of robbery, beatings, and even murder" (Bass, p. 431). Two of the texts describe lynchings of Chinese in Western towns and riots against them.

The new histories argue that if the Chinese appeared unassimilating and alien, as nativists charged, it was because they were forced to maintain a separate life in "Chinatowns" by the pressure of discrimination and the threat of violence. There the Chinese had little "opportunity to learn and adapt to the ways of living accepted by most Californians" (Todd, p. 443; Risjord, p. 462). If the Chinese had been treated more fairly, the new histories imply, they would have acculturated more readily to the surrounding society.

The Chinese, nevertheless, contributed significantly to the economic development of the far West. *"Chinese laborers made an outstanding contribution to the construction of the transcontinental railroad line.* More than 1,200 of them died building the railroads. Their often ingenious solutions to the physical barriers of the Pacific coast led one historian to say that they 'salvaged for the West millions of acres of the richest farmland and urban real estate. They could not have given more'" (Risjord, p. 462).

European Immigrants

The textbooks' accounts of immigration from Europe are more familiar, and are colored by the approbation of America's role as an asylum for the persecuted, as a land of economic opportunity, and as a tutor of democracy to European peasants who had known only despotism. The Irish fled the horrible potato famine, Germans political persecution, Jews the pogroms, and Slavs rural poverty to reach the American haven. "The experience of European immigrants in America has been both challenging and rewarding" (Linden, p. 391).

The social history of European immigrants is discussed within the two familiar groupings of "old immigrants," from northern and western Europe, who came in the mid-nineteenth century, and "new immigrants," from southern and eastern Europe, who began arriving in the late nineteenth century. Only occasionally do the texts treat individual ethnic groups such as Italians or Poles. They emphasize, therefore, the shared experiences within these broad groupings, ignoring the importance of ethnocultural differences, whether between Irish and Germans, or Jews and Italians.

Moreover, old and new immigrants alike share the basic problem of "becoming an American" (Bass, p. 427)—of assimilation, acculturation, and social mobility. "All had to find homes and work in a strange and often hostile land. Many had to learn new customs and a new language. Those who had come just a few years earlier often lent a helping hand" (Leinwand, p. 21).

American Ambivalence

All immigrants experienced a mixed reception upon arrival in the United States, since "from the beginning of its history America has been of . . . two minds about immigration" (Bass, p. 429). The need for people to settle and to develop the land encouraged a receptive attitude toward immigrants but did not eliminate fears over whether foreigners would take away land, jobs, and power from earlier Americans. "Unable to find employment, many [native] workers began to look for a scapegoat—someone upon whom they could blame their problems. The low wages offered in the United States were still higher than those offered in Europe. And immigrants who would work for low wages found jobs more easily than native-born workers. . . . As a result, native-born workers began to protest the hiring of immigrants. Often those who protested against the immigrants were people whose parents had been immigrants to the United States" (Linden, p. 309).

"Resentment against the immigrants often led to friction and violence. Riots broke out in several cities. As more immigrants arrived resentment against them increased" (Todd, p. 261). We are told that this reaction, known as "nativism," was the product of prejudice against foreign manners and appearances; it induced natives to discriminate against the newcomers in employment, education, housing, and politics. The texts discuss the Know-Nothing Party, the American Protective Association, and the Immigration Restriction League and their efforts to limit immigration and easy attainment of citizenship.

The Growth of Cities

The main theme in the textbooks' discussion of nineteenth-century European immigrants is their role in the expansion of cities and urban life. "Immigrants were especially dominant in the big cities, where they stayed in the ghettos—sections of a city in which members of a minority group live because of social, economic or legal pressure" (Leinwand, p. 21). In Risjord's account: "Before the Civil War, Irish had moved into New York and Boston, while Germans helped populate Chicago, St. Louis, and Cincinnati." The new immigrants added more ethnic communities to the big cities of the East and the Midwest. "By 1900 Chicago had more Bohemians than any other city in the world except Prague. . . . Italians, Poles, Bohemians, Croats, and Serbs worked in the steel mills of Pittsburgh, Pennsylvania and Gary, Indiana" (Risjord, p. 461). Bass writes: "It is, in fact, one of the great ironies of American life that the rapid urban growth of the late nineteenth century was mainly the product of European peasants" (Bass, p. 420). "Immigrant muscles and brains helped to transform the United States from a rural, predominantly agricultural country into an urban, industrial giant" (Todd, p. 443).

The new texts do not explore the unique cultural and social characteristics of individual immigrant groups, but they do refer in general terms to the strength of the immigrant family, the immigrant church, mutual benefit societies, and immigrant politics, all of which are shown as important factors facilitating social and economic mobility. In one case these are contrasted with the difficulties facing today's urban immigrants: "Earlier immigrants were able to use the ghetto as a springboard to success in America. Today's newcomer finds the ghetto a prison from which escape seems difficult, if not impossible" (Leinwand, p. 23).

A new view is also presented of urban politics—new, certainly, in contrast with older histories. Urban political machines based on the immigrant vote are not presented as detrimental to life in the city. Rather, they constituted a "crude welfare state," distributing jobs, money, and advice at a time when "no public welfare agencies and almost no private charities aided the newcomers" (Shenton, pp. 382, 384).

The Golden Door

The texts agree that for most immigrants America was the "golden door," an opening to a better material life, political liberties, and civil protections. Risjord remarks that "it was a rare immigrant who regretted coming" (p. 461). Successive waves of immigrants pushed groups of earlier immigrants higher up the economic scale so there was continuous social mobility. "Thus, in coal mining and many other occupations, the continuing supply of new immigrants who took jobs at the bottom of the heap provided a push upward for the immigrants who had come before" (Bass, p. 424). "Each wave of immigrants had to swallow" the "bitter pills" of "distrust and prejudice . . . but each group helped meet the needs of American development . . . [and] made their way to a better life" (Leinwand, p. 422). Even more heartening were the prospects for the next generation:

> Still more could see a better future for their children. And they were right. Thousands of sons and daughters of these immigrants became doctors, lawyers, teachers, business leaders, scientists, and government leaders (and authors of textbooks such as this) [Bass, p. 424].

The "golden door," however, began to close as new immigrants from southern and eastern Europe increasingly predominated in the influx of newcomers. More foreign in religion, customs, language, and physical appearance, they were compared unfavorably to the old immigrants, who were admired for their assimilability.

A movement toward immigration restrictions—which already banned the Chinese—was one current of a widespread reaction against minority groups as the turn of the century approached. Shenton summarizes changes in the late nineteenth century:

> The late 1800's were a bad time for American minorities. As we have seen, the states passed segregation, or "Jim Crow" laws that made black citizenship a mockery. In the same period the last organized resistance of Indian peoples was crushed, and they were penned in reservations. Finally Mexican Americans of California and the Southwest lost their lands they had held for a hundred years or more [Shenton, p. 345].

The Twentieth Century

AFTER 1900, ACCORDING TO THE TEXTS, racist theories asserting the unassimilability of the new immigrants, the demand of stronger labor unions to cut the flow of cheap immigrant workers, and political fears fueled by a Red Scare and massive strikes led to the establishment of a literacy test for entry, and, finally, in 1924, to a "national origins" quota system that discriminated against the new immigrants. "The 'wretched refuse' of foreign shores alarmed many" (Leinwand, p. 320). "The 'Golden Door' was slammed shut, and immigration fell to a trickle. It was an act of racism, reflecting the belief that Italians, Greeks, Russian Jews, and all Orientals were unworthy of becoming Americans" (Shenton, p. 488). One textbook even insists that "a quota system based on country of origin remains a feature of American immigration laws to this day" (Leinwand, p. 321). (In actuality, of course, Congress abolished the national origins quota system in 1965.)

With the ending of free immigration, little more is said about European immigrants. Most of the texts, however, assess the validity of the "melting pot" view of American society in the course of their discussions of European immigrant groups. The "melting pot" does not reckon in discussions of blacks, Indians, Asians, Mexicans, and Puerto Ricans, who are presumably regarded as standing further apart from the mainstream of American society than Europeans. Even when applied to the assimilation of European immigrants, the melting pot model is found to be deficient by three of the new histories (Leinwand, p. 425; Risjord, p. 485;

Shenton pp. 381-82). These texts describe the model as the blending together of all ethnic groups in a fiery crucible to forge a homogeneous American people out of different racial elements and ethnocultural traditions. Echoing Glazer and Moynihan in *Beyond the Melting Pot* (Cambridge, Mass., 1963), these books state that the melting pot "never worked" because ethnic groups have retained their identity and act as units for social and political action. The melting pot was more "fiction than fact," says Leinwand, for America never "melted its diverse groups into a single, unified 'mass'" (Leinwand, p. 425).

The textbook writers tend, however, to take a rather crude model of the melting pot against which to measure the reality of American society. It is feasible to hold that America *has* functioned as a melting pot, if that term is taken in a less than absolute sense to describe a society in which the mingling of cultural traits and a substantial degree of intermarriage have occurred among the various ethnic groups in the population, and in which to a great extent common values are now held by the descendants of all groups. One can criticize the extreme melting pot thesis that different peoples have merged into a new one on the basis of the obvious fact that distinct ethnic groups of European origin may still be discerned, and in some circumstances act as groups. However, the textbook writers say almost nothing of the characteristics of these surviving ethnic groups in American society and their role in American politics. More likely, the criticisms of the melting pot thesis we have referred to reflect a current ideology, one which argues that, on the basis of the experience of Indians, blacks, and Hispanic Americans, groups *should not* lose their identity in a melting pot but should survive.

BLACKS

In the texts, the early twentieth century marks both the culmination of late nineteenth-century trends toward the submergence of non-whites and Hispanic groups and the beginning of new efforts by these peoples to break the bonds of discrimination and prejudice. The texts record the beginning of black mass migration to

Northern cities during World War I, problems in finding housing and jobs, and anti-black riots during and after the war. Students are told about the creation of the NAACP, the role of W. E. B. DuBois, the Harlem Renaissance, the career of Marcus Garvey, the New Deal and its modest progress for blacks, and the major breakthroughs in presidential, judicial, and legislative action of the postwar period. In these accounts, there is a strong emphasis on the critical role of black leadership and on the importance of organizational tactics and lobbying pressure in inducing white reformers to support the civil rights movement.

The texts tell us that the social conditions in urban black ghettos declined after the industrial expansion in World War II attracted great migrations of poor blacks to urban centers in the North. "The cramped, unsanitary living conditions led to ill health, high infant death rates, high adult mortality, crime, delinquency, and the breakdown of family life" (Leinwand, p. 442). The depiction of ghetto social conditions in the new histories stresses the pathology of black life, the drug culture, criminality, and broken families, produced by discrimination and the absence of opportunity. In the "vast housing projects" of Newark's black ghetto, "crime, drugs, and poverty were an everyday part of life" (Shenton, p. 675). Leinwand asserts that "the kind of family ties that helped immigrant groups did not exist among black Americans," that black businessmen and professionals found success with difficulty because they were unable "to count on the support of their own group" as had the European immigrants, and that the unsuccessful record of black entrepreneurship was one reason why "blacks were unable to pull themselves out of the ghetto" (Leinwand, p. 424).

Poverty, social pathology, and most of all "the depth of black frustration" (Todd, p. 714) are presented as the causes of the urban riots of the 1960s. The rioters "were striking out at their environment and the hopelessness of their situation" (Risjord, p. 776; Linden, p. 664). Blacks rioted "to get the nation which, up to then, had not been listening, to hear their grievances" (Leinwand, p. 442). Although one text does say that a greater militancy among blacks and their leaders stimulated resentment and therefore contributed to violence (Linden, p. 664), all the new histories agree with the Kerner Commission that "white racism" was the chief cause of the riots.

The new histories regard with some ambivalence the rise of the Black Power movement. Stokely Carmichael, Floyd McKissick, the Black Panthers, and Malcolm X are loosely grouped as leading Black Power advocates. Some texts point out that these leaders were extremists; one refers to the "appeal to black racism" (Todd, p. 715); yet the Black Power movement is credited with significant advances for blacks. Black Power leaders are pictured as disillusioned with the gradualist approach of Martin Luther King, and as advocates of black autonomy, black pride, and potential revolutionary action. The riots, Black Power, and the expansion of black political representation end the black story. Although most of the texts take us to the election of Jimmy Carter, they say little of developments in the 1970s. Strangely, none of the texts mentions affirmative-action programs. Three of them briefly mention school busing and indicate that it has not provided clear-cut improvements in education for blacks.

When the new histories conclude by assessing the status of blacks in the 1970s, they agree that significant advances have been made, especially in politics, education, and employment (Todd, p. 716). They stress that the fight against discrimination and prejudice and the promotion of racial equality could be as difficult in the future as in the past, perhaps even more so. For example: "How to bring into existence a truly integrated society which was also color-blind remained the great unresolved question facing the American nation" (Shenton, p. 677). By implication, one can see here a reference to the problematic entitlements and special treatment that are referred to as "affirmative action."

HISPANIC AMERICANS

The texts are sensitive to the variety of groups that make up the growing category of Spanish-speaking Americans. Todd: Though the Hispanics "included several groups, each of whom differed from the others in many important ways, Spanish-speaking Americans shared certain characteristics that set them apart from the mainstream of American life." The common Hispanic heritage has been a "traditionally rural" way of life, "simple in its technology, resistant to social change, strong in its sense of group identification, and proud of its Spanish and Catholic heritage" (Todd, p. 719). Linking Mexicans and Puerto Ricans is the fact that both have "suffered prejudice and discrimination at the hands of the 'Anglo' majority" (Risjord, p. 809). To Bass, "the Mexican and Puerto Rican experience has been very much like that of earlier immigrant groups." They take poor jobs and live in poor housing but are expected, as earlier immigrants did, to rise (Bass, p. 440). Leinwand on the other hand finds Puerto Ricans most comparable to black migrants from the South: "Lacking modern industrial skills, the newcomers from Puerto Rico and the South took the unskilled jobs . . . those easily eliminated by machines or otherwise abandoned by an economy on the move"; both Puerto Ricans and blacks found "more jobs available for women than for men" (Leinwand, p. 422).

The texts attribute some of the problems of Puerto Ricans and Mexicans to their speaking Spanish. Todd writes, "The lives of young Puerto Ricans were especially difficult" because "in schools they were often handicapped by lack of bilingual programs of instruction" (Todd, p. 720). One wonders at the word "especially"—Europeans and Asians also lacked bilingual programs.

The textbooks portray Mexicans and Puerto Ricans as groups that made slow but significant social and economic gains in the last half-century but are only now beginning "to assert their identity and demand the recognition and respect their rich culture deserves" (Risjord, p. 809). Recent experiments in bilingual and bicultural school programs are cited as evidence of the gains. Bass refers to the rise of activists who "called themselves *Chicanos*" in the 1960s, demanding more opportunities and equal treatment for Mexicans, and names Jose Gutierrez and Rudolfo Gonzalez as political leaders. But Cesar Chavez stands out as "perhaps the most important leader for the masses of Mexican Americans" (Bass, p. 755). In most of the histories, Chavez is the only Mexican American mentioned, and only one text makes any reference at all to specific Puerto Ricans.

Although both Mexicans and Puerto Ricans are portrayed as undergoing painful discrimination and poverty, their experience is generally pictured as a variation of the European immigrant experience, as contrasted with blacks. For example:

> In significant ways the experiences of Puerto Ricans in the United States resembled those of earlier immigrants. Many gradually moved up the economic ladder and found places in small businesses, semi-skilled trades, the professions and the arts. . . . When the voting power of Puerto Ricans in the large cities became clear, politicians began to consider Puerto Ricans a "force" [Todd, p. 720].

According to Leinwand, the Puerto Ricans, "though following a pattern similar to that of the blacks, appear to be making headway in improving their economic and social condition." In this aspect of behavior they are likened to the Chinese and the Jews in their ability to establish "a relatively large number of small businesses" (Leinwand, p. 424)—which the text tells us blacks have been unable to accomplish.

One detects here the optimism about the Puerto Rican future found in *Beyond the Melting Pot* (1963); unfortunately, later developments have shown it was unfounded.

INDIANS

The condition of American Indians is said to have begun to improve with New Deal legislation in 1934 that halted the dissolution of reservation life. Putting a premium on ethnic-group maintenance, the texts choose to interpret federal encouragement of tribal land ownership and tribal life as a significant gain for the Indian. One praises the 1934 law for "restoring local control" and giving the Indians, "for the first time, a voice in their own destiny" (Risjord, p. 618). Another approvingly describes a halt in "the practice to make the Indians give up their age-old customs and lifestyles. Instead new emphasis was placed on teaching Indian children about their tribal culture and crafts" (Linden, p. 541). The sophisticated reader may ponder whether this program may nevertheless produce mixed effects by intensifying Indian segregation and removing Indians further from the channels of mobility and communication that existed in the surrounding society.

We are told that federal policy in the 1950s, seeking once more to "detribalize" the Indian and end the reservation system, was a "disaster" (Bass, p. 755), and its abandonment is recorded with satisfaction. The new militancy among Indian leaders is noted. Todd concludes with an account of the resilience of the Indians that is also a condemnation of white society: "By the 1970's it was evident that the Indians, once condemned as a 'vanishing race,' had not only survived but were increasing in numbers. . . . They had shown undaunted vitality and persistence in the long, bitter years of forced subordination, white patronage and chauvinism, disease, and unparalleled poverty" (Todd, p. 721).

ASIANS

The texts are interested in the Chinese and Japanese only as victims of racist immigration policies and discriminatory treatment. After 1924, when all Asian immigration was banned, the Japanese are the only Asian group discussed, and they appear because of the disaster of their incarceration in relocation camps during World War II. The story of relocation is the same in all the texts. The internment of the Japanese was the result of "an epidemic of invasion jitters" and "racial bias" (Risjord, p. 644) that produced "unjustified actions" (Todd, p. 643), and the Japanese became the "victims of the worst episode of discrimination in America since the end of slavery" (Bass, p. 441). The authors universally condemn the internment episode. No text attempts to absolve the American people or government of blame, or tries to describe the murky condition of defense intelligence and the volatility of popular sentiment toward Japan. The Japanese Americans who fought in World War II are praised for their valor in combat, which is seen as the most poignant evidence of Japanese loyalty and the injustice of mass incarceration.

None of the texts discusses perhaps the most important feature in the social history of the Japanese and the Chinese, their amazing social rise after World War II. Some discussion of this sharp change in the social and economic position of these two Asian groups, whose history of deprivation is so fully chronicled, would greatly enlarge understanding of the processes by which ethnic groups adapt and seize opportunities to better their lot. In contrast to the treatment of blacks, Indians, and Hispanics, no description is given of the culture, family, or social institutions of the Japanese, Chinese, or any other Asian group. The Asian immigrants emerge as victims and not as autonomous groups and individuals. They are instruments to dramatize the failings of policymakers and the savagery of prejudice, not human beings with a distinctive social and cultural life. Again in contrast to the treatment of blacks, Indians, and even Hispanics, we receive almost no information about outstanding Chinese Americans or Japanese Americans. One text mentions that U.S. senators Daniel Inouye and Spark Matsunaga served in the highly decorated 442nd Combat Team, and another furnishes a capsule biography of Senator S. I. Hayakawa, but these three are the only individuals mentioned.

In summary, the history of ethnic groups in the twentieth century is presented as the story of new efforts, private and public, to overcome discrimination, prejudice, and exploitation. These efforts met with some success, but the texts warn that we must guard against complacency, and that we have further to go than we have already come.

CHAPTER SIX

Civic Morality and The New History

THE NEW TREATMENT OF ETHNICITY in current textbooks changes a text from one with a single and simple national perspective to one that incorporates a variety of group perspectives. History can no longer be written from a single and unchallenged national point of view—the common stance of the past—when the histories of different ethnic groups become a major thread of historical narrative. The expansion of the American nation to the West becomes the tragedy of the Indian. The story of the South becomes the story of a great crime. The growth of industry requires the suffering of immigrants, and development of the West dispossession of the Mexican American. Whether one sees progress or not depends on the social group of which one is a member; the historian must deal with the contradiction that some groups—indeed, the central protagonists of American history—gain at the expense of others.

The addition of extensive discussions of the relations of some ethnic groups to the surrounding society make the new history textbooks, in somewhat greater measure than those of the past, histories of society rather than narratives of important events. But even with this emphasis, it should be pointed out that the major outlines of American historical development, as familiar from the texts of ten, twenty, or forty years ago, still dominate. We will find George Washington and John Adams, Andrew Jackson, Calhoun, Webster and Clay, Abraham Lincoln, Theodore Roosevelt, and Woodrow Wilson as major figures, and the central political story is not ignored, though somewhat reduced.

At some points, the major story must merge with ethnic history—after all, slavery, the Civil War, and Reconstruction have formed the central drama of American history for a long time, since long before any historian found it necessary to devote much space to the contemporary position of blacks. They still retain that place, but now the story is fuller and richer. A black perspective—as well as a Southern and a Northern perspective that we must now learn to call Southern or Northern *white*—now informs the treatment of this central drama.

Our emphasis on the treatment of race and ethnicity in these texts should not lead readers to assume undue neglect of the major themes of American history. One finds in these texts the story of colonial settlement, the Revolution, the development of our political institutions, the westward expansion of the United States, industrial expansion, the nation's role in world affairs since the Spanish American War and World War I, and other central themes of American history. After all, our count of pages devoted to racial and ethnic groups showed a range from as little as 5.4 and 5.6 per cent to a maximum of 10.4 and 11.6 per cent. That does not seem to us to represent undue attention to racial and ethnic groups.

History as a Success Story

The issue is rather that the new elements of social and ethnic history do not merge easily with the old, in part because of the way they are treated. General American history, as is true of all national histories for younger students, is treated primarily as a success story. It is never suggested that the Revolution, or the Civil War, or the westward expansion, or our becoming a world power, or our policy of free immigration, were mistakes—though doubts have often been expressed, and continue to be, on the wisdom or morality of the Mexican-American War, the Spanish-American War, and now, also, the Vietnam War.

The incorporation of nineteenth-century European immigrant groups into American society can also be treated as a success. But Indians, blacks, and Hispanic minorities, groups that dominate the discussion of racial and ethnic minorities in history texts, raise more difficult problems of incorporation. Their stories form a running contradiction to the prevailing optimistic account. If a textbook observes, as one does, that in the late nineteenth-century era of industrial expansion "a prosperous society was developing in the United States," it must also point out that "minorities were pushed to the edges of the nation's life" (Shenton, p. 345). The new American history, with its multiple perspectives and its varied peoples with drastically different fates, is a troubled one. Given the elements that make it up, the new histories cannot inculcate a simple patriotism based on a unitary concept of American nationality and of American interests.

A New Civic Morality

The new histories are emphatically not simple patriotic history, in which all blemishes and problems are ignored. Instead, we see a new civic morality whose major ingredients are understanding, sympathy, and respect for the humanity of all ethnic minorities. By describing the social and cultural history of ethnic groups, the texts supply what might be called a basic level of "ethnic literacy." But it is very basic indeed. It emphasizes the positive features of each group, and elicits sympathy by vividly picturing the efforts of ethnic minorities to defend themselves from discrimination and to advance under inhospitable circumstances. Inevitably, this emphasis on discrimination and prejudice and on the struggle against oppression reduces the stature of the "white" majority, still the main protagonist of these histories. And the fact that the new texts have as yet found no way of incorporating any sophisticated or complex view of the white European immigrants of the nineteenth and twentieth centuries inevitably sharpens the disjunction between oppressors and oppressed, and tends on occasion to reduce American history to only that.

There is indeed a history of oppressors and oppressed, and it must be told. But the white "oppressors" themselves form a complex mix of European ethnic groups, divided by language and religion. Almost all these groups, too, have their own story to tell of encountering discrimination and prejudice. And yet almost all of them have experienced over time better education, higher incomes, jobs of higher status, and participation in the common political life of the United States. And this is, increasingly, the experience of the non-white groups.

A somewhat greater attention to the European ethnic groups would thus help bridge the radical disjunction the student finds in these texts between an oppressive white majority and heroic, oppressed non-white minorities. The old myths of racism, which were prominent in American texts of the twenties and thirties, are now replaced by new myths proclaiming the superior moral qualities of minorities, and we find a Manichaean inversion in which whites are malevolent and blacks, Indians, Asians, and Hispanics are tragic victims. Both sides are human, with all that entails, and we feel this humanity would come into better focus if there were greater attention to European ethnic groups, who both have been the victims of American nativism and the religious prejudices of dominant Protestants and have, in time, without surrendering their identity or changing their religions, become incorporated into a "white" majority. They complicate the history of this white majority. They indicate to students where *they* might fit into the story of the American people—something that a radical disjunction between racist whites and victimized non-white minorities does not easily permit for many students. And they offer a bridge of varied experiences between those of early and dominant white settlers and those of non-white victims, native, imported, or free immigrants. In providing such a bridge of experiences, they also indicate a potential course for those non-white minorities and new immigrants— increasingly non-white—who may still range below the mean in education, income, and influence.

Doing Justice to Diversity

We suggest this somewhat increased emphasis as a matter not of giving "equal time" to all components of the American population—something that is probably impossible and would anyway be pointlessly divisive—but of presenting a more complex, and truer, picture of American diversity, and of the problems and successes of the American political system in dealing with it. The American story cannot be properly reduced to that of exploited and exploiters; yet this is what the concentration on the non-white minorities and their tribulations must inevitably mean. The problem is one that other histories, and historians, have faced. Can the history of Christianity be reduced to martyrology, followed by the triumph of truth? Or the history of the Jews to that of massacre? Both Christian and Jewish historians have fought this type of reduction. Today, the most sensitive historians of American minority groups also protest such a picture. Textbook writers should be following them.

Ultimately, when textbooks portray the history of ethnic groups as a repeated struggle between victims and oppressors—between subject and dominant peoples—the central processes that integrated American society are trivialized. Since the textbooks dwell on ethnic groups as antagonists, the new history fails to show their joint participation in historical movements that created a fluid and pluralistic social system. For example, the student receives no sense of the impact of public schooling on the mobility of ethnic groups, of the relation of black migration to public efforts to combat discrimination, or of the role of immigrants in broadening American religious institutions. In concentrating narrowly on ethnic conflict, the new history slights the forces that have created common bases of group experience and group interests that transcended ethnic lines.

Many of the historiographical weaknesses in the new history texts stem from the flawed assumption that American society has been a rigid mosaic of ethnic groups, each static and separate. The textbooks overlook the looseness of American ethnic relations, the voluntary nature of ethnic affiliation, and the need of ethnic groups to form linkages with outsiders to promote their interests, all of which have made ethnicity a dynamic factor in social change, not a category under which all historical process can be subsumed.

Two Other Textbooks

In chapter one we mentioned two textbooks that give more space to ethnic and minority issues than the six we examined. Charles G. Sellers's document-based *As It Happened* devotes extended space to European minority groups (in particular, Irish and Jews) and to Asians (in particular, Japanese), and also gives full accounts of American Indians, blacks, and Mexican Americans. This attention, and this text's resort to original documents, are admirable; but the use to which these advanced techniques are put is dismaying. The reader learns only of anti-Semitism, nothing of the remarkable economic, social, and political rise of Jews in the United States. He is given an extended account of Japanese Americans' relocation, but he hears nothing about their remarkable educational and economic success, their entry into politics, their social acceptance. He reads of trade union discrimination but is told nothing about the varied programs that are increasing black representation in skilled trades.

The second text, *The American Adventure*, from the Educational Research Council of America, is better balanced. Without being ethnocentric, it says that the Aztecs governed their subjects with "grim efficiency" and refers to their religion as "gory" (A80). It breathes the same sympathy for the American Indians and their tragic fate as all the other texts we have discussed but does not hesitate to refer to Indian as well as white massacres (B192, C177-78), or to the fact that Indians tortured their prisoners (A62). It deals with the new immigrants from Europe and Asia in a widely ranging chapter entitled "The Melting Pot and the Challenge of Group Relations," and its conclusion on "the peoples of America" ends not on the note of still unmodified prejudice and discrimination but with the complex problems raised by a multi-ethnic society in which groups have advanced (or not) at different rates and in which the issues of national and group identity and loyalty raise difficult problems. Its treatment of school busing and affirmative action is one that students will have no difficulty relating to, for these matters are presented as controversial and troublesome.

The over-simple language and large type of this text are not to our taste—in these respects we prefer Sellers. But in one respect, quite apart from the new issues of race and ethnicity, *The American Adventure* marks a departure, and that is by restoring more of the narrative history of the past. Its wars do include battles—and they are described, with the battlegrounds presented in maps. One point of particular interest to us is that this text records an event in early American history that was used by Bessie Pierce fifty years ago as a test of prejudice against Spanish Catholics: the massacre by the Spaniard Menendez of the French Huguenot colony in Florida. Alas, when we reviewed our six texts to find out how *they* treated this matter, we could find no reference to it in any of them. The event had disappeared in the general and radical reduction of incident and narrative in American history. Although the account in *The American Adventure* cannot, unfortunately, match the drama, even if romantic and sentimental, that was once common in the American history textbook, the incident is there.

Exploitation as the Essence

Today, in view of the dominant political orientation of American social scientists, more extended treatments of race and ethnicity will probably mean more of what we found in the six texts we examined—an emphasis on victimization, on discrimination, on prejudice, giving the clear impression that the essence of the United States' relation to race and ethnicity has been exploitation. Indeed, the most likely outcome is a picture of a great exploiter and a host of victims—Indians, blacks, Asians, Latin Americans, and others. One thus fears that the first effect of greater attention to minority and immigrant groups in American texts, and of an effort to integrate them into American history, will be simply to spread a view of this country as exploitative, unequal, and almost unredeemable in its general nastiness. The Sellers volume ends with the dangers of the CIA and the environmental crisis, and one wonders, must we pass through such a one-sided view of American history in order to incorporate a more realistic and rounded view of race and ethnicity?

It is hard to believe that such one-sided approaches will do much to engage students. They live in a world in which busing is an ever-present reality, and affirmative action is a major issue affecting almost every civil servant and employee of a major organization; a world in which Democrats and Republicans alike eschew harsh and punitive measures in dealing with illegal immigration; a world in which they see Asian schoolmates advancing and new Asian immigrants beginning to progress through the cycles of past immigrants. What will they then make of histories that speak only of victims and exploiters when they deal with racial and ethnic minorities? Students can approach such histories only, one feels, with skepticism and incomprehension—or, if they put aside their living experience, they can only fall victim to misleading sophisticated ideologies.

There are thus distortions, oversimplifications, misplaced emphases, and simple absences in the new texts, despite their efforts to progress from the kind of barely conscious racism and ethnocentrism that was accepted with little question a few decades ago. They have modest virtues. They seek to engage the student's conscience in the ongoing process of creating a society that provides social justice for all ethnic groups. They undermine the complacency of students and try to replace it with an understanding, sympathy, and respect for all ethnic groups.

But at the moment, they seem overzealous and unsteady in making concrete a new and important direction in the interpretation of American history. One hopes that as textbook writers continue to incorporate information and understanding about ethnic and racial minorities in subsequent editions of these and other texts, they will ask themselves whether they show the history of American society to be so flawed by racism and discrimination that they obscure the considerable institutional and social achievements of the American polity. For after all, one must ask whether further progress will be aided or hampered by the guilt and self-reproach the students of these books must and are intended to feel, or by the false sense of moral superiority that will be induced by imposing the standards of today on the historical actors in our past.

Index of Names

ETHICS AND PUBLIC POLICY REPRINTS

Reprints are $1 each. Postpaid if payment accompanies order.
Orders of $20 or more, 10 per cent discount.